A VISIONARY OF POLICE REFORM IN COMPLEX TIMES

SHERIFF LEE BACA

KAREN RICHARDSON

THE
MENTORIS
PROJECT

The author has made every effort to ensure the accuracy of the information within this book was correct at time of publication. The author does not assume and hereby disclaims any liability to any party for any loss, damage, or disruption caused by errors or omissions, whether such errors or omissions result from accident, negligence, or any other cause.

Mentoris Project
745 South Sierra Madre Drive
San Marino, CA 91108

Copyright © 2022 Mentoris Project

Cover photo: REUTERS / Alamy Stock Photo
Map courtesy of https://d-maps.com/carte.php?num_car=36329&lang=en

Quotations at beginning of each chapter by Lee Baca

More information at www.mentorisproject.org

ISBN: 978-1-947431-51-5

Library of Congress Control Number: 2022943083

All rights reserved, which includes the right to reproduce this book or portions thereof in any form whatsoever except as provided by the U.S. Copyright Law. For information address the Mentoris Project

All net proceeds from the sale of this book will be donated to the Mentoris Project, whose mission is to support educational initiatives that foster an appreciation of history and culture to encourage and inspire young people to create a stronger future.

Publisher's Cataloging-in-Publication (Provided by Cassidy Cataloguing Services, Inc.)
Names: Richardson, Karen, (Biographical novelist), author.
Title: Sheriff Lee Baca : a visionary of police reform in complex times / Karen Richardson.
Description: San Marino, CA : The Mentoris Project, [2022] | Includes bibliographical references.
Identifiers: ISBN: 978-1-947431-51-5 | LCCN: 2022943083
Subjects: LCSH: Baca, Lee. | Sheriffs--California--Los Angeles County--Biography. | Law enforcement--California--Los Angeles County. | Civil rights--California--Los Angeles County. | Los Angeles (Calif.)--Race relations. | LCGFT: Biographies.
Classification: LCC: HV7911.B23 R53 2022 | DDC: 363.282092--dc23

Contents

Foreword	i
Chapter 1: East L.A.	1
Chapter 2: The Grinder	15
Chapter 3: The Starting Line	25
Chapter 4: Two Gold Bars	37
Chapter 5: Tour De Force	53
Chapter 6: Community Building	69
Chapter 7: Taking the Plunge	79
Chapter 8: Trust	89
Chapter 9: A Life Worth Living	117
Chapter 10: Faith and Heroism	135
Chapter 11: Cooperation and Global Diplomacy	145
Chapter 12: The Sting and the Judge	155
Epilogue: La Tuna Federal Correctional Institution	179
Appendix A	183
Appendix B	207
Appendix C	210
Appendix D	214
Sources	215

When I was a young man, I wanted to change the world.
I found it was difficult to change the world, so I tried to change my nation.
When I found I couldn't change the nation, I began to focus on my town.
I couldn't change the town, and as an older man, I tried to change my family.
Now, as an old man, I realize the only thing I can change is myself, and suddenly I realize that if long ago I had changed myself, I could have made an impact on my family.
My family and I could have made an impact on our town.
Their impact could have changed the nation and I could indeed have changed the world.

—Written by an unknown monk around 1100 A.D.

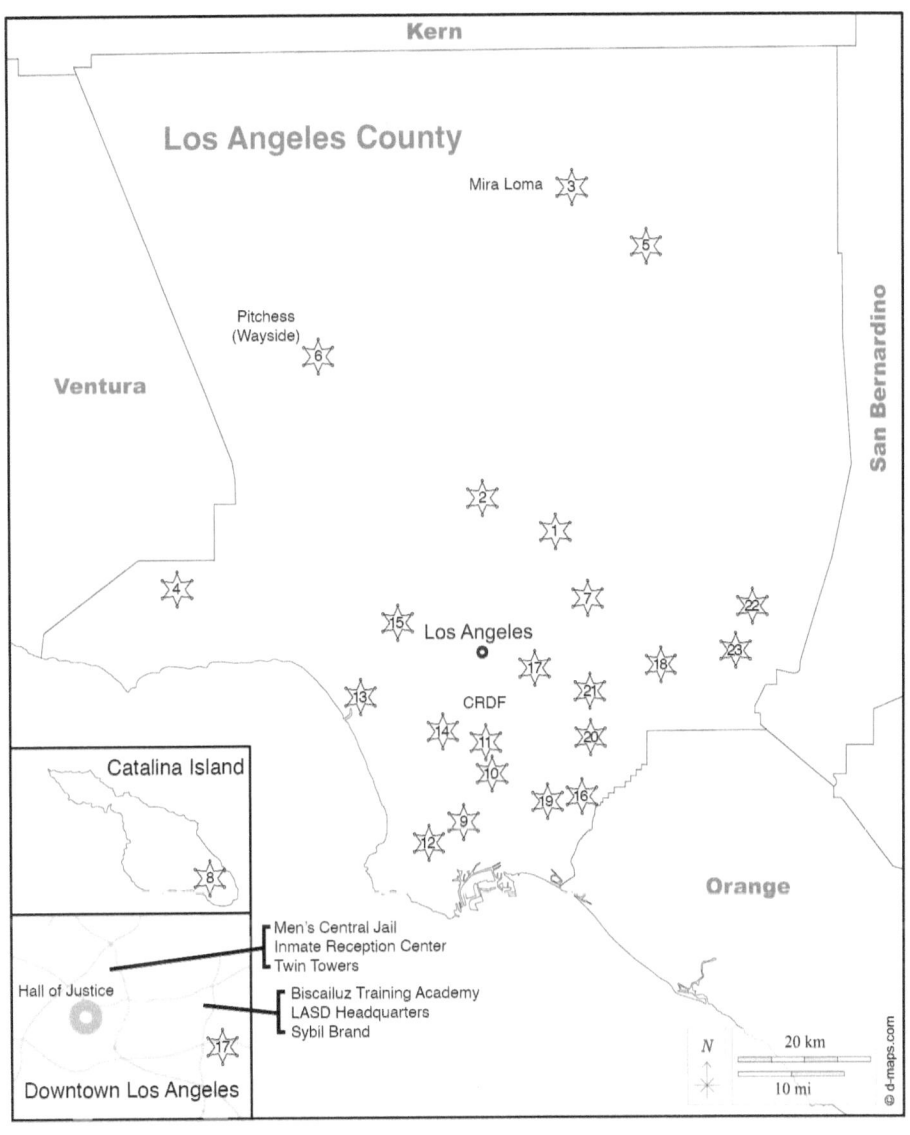

LASD STATIONS AND JAILS, 2014

REGION I

1. Altadena
2. Crescenta Valley
3. Lancaster
4. Malibu / Lost Hills
5. Palmdale
6. Santa Clarita Valley
7. Temple

REGION II

8. Avalon
9. Carson
10. Century
11. Compton
12. Lomita
13. Marina del Rey
14. South L.A.
15. West Hollywood

REGION III

16. Cerritos
17. East L.A.
18. Industry
19. Lakewood
20. Norwalk
21. Pico Rivera
22. San Dimas
23. Walnut / Diamond Bar

Foreword

As I write this, police are under attack like never before. Protestors across the United States want to abolish the police, or at the very least, defund them. Demonstrations that started peacefully have been upended by agitators and quickly escalated into chaos with looting, violence, arson, and loss of life. Sometimes it feels like the news channels are just replaying old footage. Incident after incident, it's the same scene: Paramilitary-outfitted police in shoulder-to-shoulder formation behind ballistic shields trying to deflect hurled bricks and bottles as they attempt to subdue and break up a raging mob. Launching tear gas and flash-bang grenades, shooting beanbag rounds and rubber bullets, their faces remain unseen behind their protective gas masks. They look almost like a robotic force from a dystopian movie.

But strip away the protective gear and you'll see human beings who are as flawed and scared as the rest of us. Whether pulling over a motorist, mitigating a domestic dispute, knocking on a stranger's door, or quelling a riot, they always need to be prepared for the worst. When confronting people who are already in a heightened state and feel like they have nothing left to lose—whether from drugs, alcohol, anger, fear, or mental illness—there's no telling who might be armed and one trigger-pull away from ending the lives of those who try to intervene.

SHERIFF LEE BACA

Sworn to protect and serve the public, and knowingly putting their own lives in danger, cops begin their shifts on the streets and in the courts or jails, never knowing what horrors await. They're often the first responders to unspeakable tragedies and witnesses to the dying and the dead. Death by natural causes, self-inflicted gunshot wounds, hangings, overdoses, drownings, car crashes, train crashes, school shootings, drive-by shootings, domestic violence disputes, and terrorist attacks . . . bodies pumping out their last ccs of blood and bodies that have been undiscovered for days. And then there are the children. I can't even bring myself to think about that.

After dealing with one of these gruesome events, an officer might then find himself or herself consoling a rape victim, trying to talk a jumper off a freeway overpass, informing parents about the death of their child, or settling a disturbance between two neighbors. If the skills needed to transition from extreme emotional situations to the most mundane—on the turn of a dime—don't inspire awe, appreciation, and humility in you, I don't know what will.

Now, I don't deny there are badge-heavy officers prone to bribery, corruption, and excessive brutality. When I was six years old, I shined shoes on Jamaica Avenue in Queens, New York. Underage and unlicensed, I was frequently harassed and chased by police. When a cop smashed my box with his baton, there went my ten-cents-a-polish enterprise. By no means am I equating my experience with the unprovoked shootings and chokehold deaths of today. My point is that police officers are as different from each other as all human beings are. We're all subject to making poor decisions and failing under pressure. Unfortunately, the irrevocable mistakes police make are too often a matter of life and death.

I still believe it is a noble profession, and in my mind, no one exemplifies it more than Sheriff Lee Baca.

From birth, the odds of Lee doing anything productive with his life were slim. Born Mexican American in a Los Angeles barrio to a mother

FOREWORD

who was illegally brought into the United States and to a father who abandoned the family before his son was a year old, Lee's was a less than fortuitous start in life. At eleven months old, he suffered an injury in a severe accident that took over four years to heal. And when he was seven, his overwhelmed mother decided to keep her daughter and youngest son but put Lee up for adoption. Statistically, Lee was "high-risk," prone to a future of juvenile delinquency, problems in school, and gang life.

When I first heard the sheriff speak, I was immediately struck by his goodness, empathy, intelligence, faith, and philosophical opinions on all aspects of life. True public servants are a rare breed these days, and he epitomized everything one should be. The Los Angeles County Sheriff's Department's motto is "A Tradition of Service." Lee Baca's could well be "A *Lifetime* of Service."

Lee's service to his fellow man can be traced back to when his mother left him. That year, he moved in with his paternal grandparents and immediately began helping them care for his severely disabled adult uncle, with whom he shared a small bedroom.

While in high school Lee served as senior class president and began a lifetime of volunteer work.

From there, Lee served his country when he joined the Marine Corps Reserve.

As a husband and father of two, Lee served his family.

At twenty-three, Lee swore in as a Los Angeles County sheriff's deputy and served the area's citizens for forty-eight years.

For many of those years, Lee served as a junior high, high school, and college teacher.

Lee served as a mentor, counselor, social worker, and disciplinarian, and, when sheriff, commanded the largest sheriff's department in the country, overseeing a $2.5 billion budget, over eighteen thousand sworn and civilian staff, and the nation's largest jail system of twenty thousand inmates.

SHERIFF LEE BACA

After the 9/11 attacks, Lee served the state of California as a regional coordinator of Mutual Aid Emergency Services.

Lee served the nation and the Muslim community by testifying in front of the House of Representative's Homeland Security Committee to promote healing and communication and to reduce racial discrimination.

Traveling overseas, Lee served the international community by sharing his community policing ideas with leaders and law enforcement agencies.

Somehow, Lee still made the time to serve on numerous nonprofits' boards of directors.

Rarely carrying a gun, Lee Baca sees himself as more of a social worker than the long arm of the law. Regardless of one's race, creed, sexuality, or economic circumstance, he wants to help. When he looks you in the eye, you feel like you're the only person in the room. He makes you feel that no matter what, everything's going to be okay. In Lee's view, the MS-13 gang member, the Malibu movie star, and everyone in between are God's creatures, and Lee's purpose in life is to help them however he can.

Lee sees the best in people, even in the worst.

When Lee and I first sat in my living room to discuss this book, he had been convicted of obstruction of justice and was waiting for the decision on his second appeal. If he lost, he would serve his sentence in federal prison. Though mostly cogent and engaged, there were times I could see signs of his deteriorating condition from Alzheimer's disease. He said he still ran every day as he had for forty years, but now did word puzzles too to exercise his brain.

As he was leaving my house, it was as if Lee read the question on my mind I wouldn't dare ask: What if he lost the appeal?

Resolute, he volunteered that he had no fear or anxiety about going to prison should it come to that. He was confident he could handle it, and the potential loss of creature comforts was of no concern to him.

FOREWORD

In a strange way, it almost felt that he embraced the idea of being incarcerated and part of him was actually looking forward to the challenge. I sensed that not much rattled Lee and that he would use the time to serve both his jailers and fellow internees. I knew all would be changed for the better for having served alongside him.

I wanted to publish this book because it was clear to me that Lee was made a scapegoat, a poster boy for police brutality in these anti-police times, laden with the sins of all the corrupt, racist, out-of-bounds cops who have been tarnishing the profession for decades—cops who are everything Lee isn't and never was.

Cancel culture and sensationalist soundbites are destroying people's lives. Who among us would hold up to the scrutiny where we are uniformly judged on our mistakes, all good deeds and accomplishments forgotten?

I hope that after reading Lee's story, you will come to respect the man I know him to be. And the next time someone is under attack, I hope you will step out of the echo chamber and put in the due diligence to learn the whole story. Isn't that what we would all hope for should we ever find ourselves in their shoes?

—Robert Barbera

Chapter 1

East L.A.

"Kindness is actually the greatest strength on Earth."

In the early morning hours of Sunday, August 2, 1942, twenty-two-year-old farmworker José Díaz lay dying on a dirt road near a popular swimming hole known as Sleepy Lagoon. Surrounded by cornfields, the reservoir on the Williams Ranch in what is now Commerce, California, was popular with young Mexican American Angelenos. By day, the idyllic spot offered teens denied access to "Whites Only" public swimming pools relief from the blistering desert sun. By night, it provided lovestruck couples an escape from the overcrowded apartments they shared with their large families in the barrios.

On August 1, Hank Leyvas had brought his girlfriend to Sleepy Lagoon for such an interlude. Strains of live music from a nearby birthday party for a woman named Amelia Delgadillo carried through the still air to their car. But any romantic intentions Leyvas might have had abruptly ended when members of a local gang from Downey chanced upon the couple. Adrenalized after crashing and creating trouble at the birthday party, the boys were primed for more action. Taunting Leyvas and his girlfriend, their verbal insults quickly led to blows, and the young lovers were both badly beaten.

Humiliated and enraged—and a gang member himself—Leyvas returned to his neighborhood in South Los Angeles to corral his pals from the 38th Street gang. Hell-bent on revenge, the fourteen- to twenty-two-year-old zoot suit–clad pachucos caravanned to Sleepy Lagoon to look for the boys who had attacked Leyvas. For the second time that night, hot-tempered punks upended Amelia Delgadillo's birthday party. The band had packed up around one a.m., so the remaining guests were dancing in the backyard to music from a radio. Inebriated and armed with knives, clubs, and chains, the boys from 38th Street arrived looking for revenge, and though the Downey gang was long gone, they tangled with both male and female partygoers in a short but violent brawl.

A few boys from 38th Street missed the start of the melee at the Delgadillo ranch house. While on their way, they veered off the road and got stuck in a ditch near Sleepy Lagoon. Their girlfriends got out to help push the car free. On the dirt road, bathed in the light of the not-quite-full moon, was a young man bleeding from his head and mouth, his fists and face swollen and cut, his skull fractured. His breath was shallow. He was unconscious. The pockets of his baggy pants were turned inside out. The girls tried to assess his condition and offer assistance, but their boyfriends pulled them away, eager to join the action at the Delgadillo home. The young man was José Díaz, who lived in a bunkhouse on the Williams Ranch and had been a guest at the birthday party. After being discovered by a Good Samaritan, Díaz died a few hours later at Los Angeles County General Hospital from a subdural hemorrhage. It was supposed to have been his first day serving in the US Army.

A decade before José Díaz's murder, the country was in the throes of the Great Depression. Three of every four working Americans were unemployed. Charities struggled to feed the poverty-stricken in breadlines that stretched for city blocks. Despair had become the nation's ethos.

President Herbert Hoover wanted to put a chicken in every pot and get Americans back to work. When he stated that Mexicans "took jobs away from American citizens," he hit a nerve with the public. In 1931, the government began forcibly repatriating Mexican aliens. It is estimated that up to a million were deported, 60 percent of whom were actually US citizens. In one raid at a Los Angeles park, immigration agents rounded up around four hundred unsuspecting men and women onto dozens of flatbed trucks consigned for the train station. Over the next five years, approximately one-third of Los Angeles's Mexican population was deported. When the Los Angeles City Council complained to the County Board of Supervisors, they got this response: "This isn't about constitutional validity. It's about the color of their skin."

Absurdly, the government flip-flopped on its policy a few years later. Now at war, the country faced a labor shortage caused when men of working age joined the military to fight the Germans and Japanese. Days after Díaz was murdered, the federal government signed a bilateral labor agreement with Mexico to offset the loss of farmworkers. The Bracero Program offered incentives for Mexican laborers to come work in America. In the decade that followed, the Mexican population in Los Angeles soared to approximately 250,000.

The year 1942 was a time of exceptional racial tension in the City of Angels. Distrust of the "other" was rampant. The US government had begun incarcerating Japanese Americans at the Manzanar War Relocation Center two hundred miles north of Sleepy Lagoon. Of those detainees, 90 percent came from Los Angeles. Posters and pamphlets spread messages such as "How to Spot a Jap," "Stay on the Job Until Every Murdering Jap is Wiped Out!," and "Don't Speak the Enemy's Language, Speak American."

While Mexican men and women toiled in the fields, their children grew up largely unsupervised in barrios cut off from other Angelenos. Segregated by their neighborhoods and poverty, as well as direct ordinances (and some by their language), disaffected young men found camaraderie in a growing gang culture. The Los Angeles Police Department (LAPD) was trying to get the upper hand on Mexican gangs. Its best and most experienced officers had joined the military and left to fight for their country. Those who remained were less experienced and fell short of their duty to protect and to serve. Additionally, the situation with the Mexican gangs had created a public relations ordeal, partly of the LAPD's own making. The *Los Angeles Examiner*, a branch of William Randolph Hearst's syndicate, was thriving by publishing lurid and sensational headlines to sell more newspapers, and the LAPD had been feeding the beast exaggerated accounts of the crimes committed by Mexican gangs. Further hyperbole from tabloid reporters instilled a fear of violence in the public that far outweighed the gangs' actual threat. On a different day, the death of José Díaz—to too many, "just another Mexican"—might have gone unnoticed or been written off as inconsequential. But the LAPD had decided it needed to show they had the "Mexican problem" under control. They needed to make a statement.

Instead of investigating the murder and interviewing witnesses however, the LAPD rounded up between three to six hundred boys and young men in an unprecedented citywide dragnet. All the detainees were of Mexican descent. When they discovered Hank Leyvas had been at Sleepy Lagoon the night of the murder, they arrested him and twenty-one members of the 38th Street gang. The police already knew Leyvas and they didn't like him; the cocky nineteen-year-old had been in trouble before. The first time was when he'd been arrested for car theft and spent three days in jail until his father found the title slip showing that the car was actually his, as he'd been saying all along. Leyvas had also been arrested for loitering, fighting, armed robbery, assault with

CHAPTER 1

a deadly weapon, and assault and battery. In Leyvas the LAPD had found its scapegoat. And in the trial that followed—whether or not it was a spoken agreement—the district attorney's office and judge who heard the case decided they too would make an example out of Hank Leyvas. The "Mexican problem" needed a face and Leyvas fit the bill.

The judge wouldn't let the seventeen accused gang members sit with their attorneys or change their clothes for the trial. The once immaculately groomed pack sat in the courtroom in the glad rags they'd been wearing for weeks, now bloody, dirty, and torn from their scuffle in Sleepy Lagoon, as well as from the beatings they'd received from the police while in custody. The judge said he wanted the jury to see them for who they really were. Despite no police investigation, an overwhelming lack of evidence, and conflicting testimony from witnesses, on January 12, 1943, all but five of the accused gang members, including Leyvas, were found guilty of the murder of José Díaz. They were sent to San Quentin prison, four hundred miles away from their working-class families. Their "leader," Hank Leyvas, got a life sentence. Five girls who had refused to cooperate were declared wards of the state, and though they had no trial, they were sent to the dreaded Ventura School for Girls facility.

Angelenos of Mexican heritage were crushed by the verdict, which intensified their distrust of the police after years of harassment at their hands. Other Angelenos believed the pachucos had it coming. On a more positive note, a group of activists and concerned citizens, including Orson Welles, Rita Hayworth, and Anthony Quinn, helped the boys from 38th Street overturn the verdict, and all were released after serving close to two years in prison. Their pachuca girlfriends, however, were held in reform school until they turned twenty-one.

Before the Dodgers moved from Brooklyn to Los Angeles and claimed the land to build a baseball stadium, Chavez Ravine was a barrio. Thousands of Mexican Americans lived there and in the surrounding enclaves. During the war, servicemen from around the country rotated through the area's newly built Navy and Marine Corps Reserve Armory. Terrified of their fate yet fired up to annihilate the enemy on the other side of the Pacific, boys barely out of high school understood that whether they survived or perished, their time in Los Angeles would be the end of life as they knew it. Downtown jazz bars beckoned, offering booze, dancing, and a chance to meet a girl or two.

Stigmatized and distrusted by those who held all the power, younger Mexicans became protective of the precious little they could call their own. Outside their barrios they saw signs like "We Serve Whites Only—No Spanish or Mexicans." Their hostility toward the outside world and the police who continually harassed them grew to include the cocksure uniformed boys who eyed their girlfriends and swaggered drunkenly through *their* streets.

Barrio gangs had cultivated a new look, adopting the comically oversized zoot suits worn by Cab Calloway and popularized by the dance-hall crowd. For jitterbuggers, the billowing pants provided freedom of movement and the tapered ankles kept them from tripping over their hems. For the pachucos, the voluminous knee-length jackets easily concealed chains, clubs, and other weapons and were an extravagance otherwise lacking in their lives. The fashion spread beyond the gangs throughout the Mexican community.

But outside that community, resentment over the zoot suit was building. War rations were in effect. The growing list of limited items included gasoline, coffee, sugar, silk stockings, and the wool needed for soldiers' uniforms. The War Production Board issued regulations on clothing that essentially banned the manufacture of zoot suits because of their wasteful use of fabric. But like any outlawed product, the outfits were still available on the black market, with some sellers even offering installment plans.

To the new enlistees who were sacrificing everything they held dear to protect the freedom and liberty of others—including the pachucos who heckled them—the baggy zoot suits were seen as a blatant contempt for their service.

No defining historical incident is borne in a vacuum. With the benefit of hindsight, we can connect a sequence of events and see it was just a matter of time before all hell was going to break loose. Four months after the Sleepy Lagoon trial, the fuse was lit on the night of May 30, 1943, when a few sailors and pachucos passed each other in the Alpine barrio near Chavez Ravine. A fight broke out, leaving one of the sailors with a broken jaw.

Just as the 38th Street gang members had searched for the Downey gang to avenge Hank Leyvas's beating, sixteen sailors from the armory—carrying belts and clubs—went looking for the "drapes" who had beaten one of their own. The Zoot Suit Riots had begun.

The next night, fifty sailors joined the fray. The following night, two hundred. And over the weekend, five thousand civilians and servicemen—some from the army and marine corps on shore leave, others who bused into the city from San Diego and Las Vegas—went on a search-and-destroy mission through downtown and the barrios of East Los Angeles. A couple of twelve- and thirteen-year-old boys were pulled from a movie theater and left on the street as the clothing deemed so offensive was ripped from their bodies and burned in a pile next to them. Night after night, the mayhem escalated. When the mob couldn't find zoot-suiters, they began attacking any Mexican they could find, as well as Italians, Filipinos, and African Americans.

Newspapers continued to inflame the situation with headlines like "Zoot Suiters Learn Lesson in Fights with Servicemen" and "Pachuco Gangs Tangle in New Street Brawls with Navy; Cry 'Death to Cops.'" The LAPD was later chastised for sitting back while the city they were sworn to protect and serve imploded. Some had even joined the fight. When the police did show up to make arrests, it was after the servicemen had left the area. Thus, after five nights of unbridled violence, most of the five hundred people detained were Mexican. The military finally declared the city of Los Angeles off-limits to all personnel and put an end to the Zoot Suit Riots on June 8, 1943. Surprisingly, no lives were lost.

This was the Los Angeles of Leroy "Lee" Baca's infancy.

Boyle Heights is a neighborhood east of downtown Los Angeles. Today it can be found where the 5, 10, 60, and 101 freeways meet. With over half a million vehicles passing through every day, the tangle of concrete and asphalt known as the "Spaghetti Bowl" is the busiest interchange in the world. But in 1943 in the days of trolleys and buses, twelve-lane freeways were as unimaginable as the outlandish notion that the miles of blacktop wouldn't be enough to accommodate the number of automobiles Angelenos would accumulate. Some Boyle Heights streets were paved, some were not. The multicultural neighborhood was one of the only areas in Los Angeles without restricted housing covenants that discriminated against people of color. The diverse enclave was home to approximately five thousand Japanese Americans, thirty-five thousand Jews, and fifteen thousand Mexican Americans—including Thomas and Consuelo (née Hernandez) Baca and their two children: three-year-old Elaine and one-year-old Leroy David—known as Lee—born on May 27, 1942.

On June 6, 1943, the Zoot Suit Riots had spread into Boyle Heights and come within a mile and a half of 1020 Bonnie Beach Place, where the Bacas shared a one-bedroom apartment. Infant Lee was still in excruciating pain from a dreadful accident. Two months earlier, he'd been crawling under the ironing board and become tangled in the iron's electrical cord. The hot iron fell onto Lee's right knee, searing deep into his skin. The wound failed to heal and secreted a foul-smelling, purulent fluid for years. The constant pain limited the boy's ability to crawl and, later, to walk and run.

When Lee was three years old, his father enlisted in the US Navy. World War II was over, and Tom only served a year. But instead of

CHAPTER 1

coming home after his assignment, Tom offered Consuelo $15 a month in child support and filed for divorce.

When he was five, Lee's mother took him to Children's Hospital for surgery, where doctors grafted skin from his left thigh to his right knee. When he woke up from anesthesia, both his legs were in casts and would remain so for two weeks. Unable to take time off work, Consuelo couldn't visit her son and Lee worried she would never come back for him. For as long as he could remember, pain had been a daily part of Lee's life. He thought he knew what pain was—but that was until they removed his casts. To this day, he describes the process as unbearable, saying, "This encounter gave me the courage to endure physical pain and believe it would pass."

Born in Mexico, Consuelo's parents had illegally brought her into the United States when she was an infant. A single mother, she would bring Lee and Elaine to school, then take the bus to a downtown clothing factory, where she worked as a seamstress. Already overwhelmed, when she gave birth to a third child, she couldn't cope. Something had to give. And for reasons known only to her, she decided that something was her then seven-year-old son. Consuelo put Lee up for adoption.

When Clara Baca, Lee's paternal grandmother, found out, she was outraged. She insisted Lee come live with her, his grandfather Tomas, and their disabled adult son. Consuelo dropped Lee off at her in-laws' and told him she would come back for him the next day. She didn't. Nor would she.

Clara's family, the Bottoms, came from Perryville, Kentucky, where they had settled long before approximately thirty-eight thousand Union and Confederate soldiers had clashed on the family farm in the Battle of Perryville, one of the bloodiest of the Civil War. After the war, Clara's father, Charles Bottom, had moved to the New Mexico Territory, where silver ore had recently been discovered. There he helped establish Silver City, met his Mexican-born wife, and likely frequented the same saloons as Billy the Kid, Butch Cassidy, and the Wild Bunch. Charles and his wife had three children. Their only daughter, Clara, married Tomas Baca, a hardworking boilermaker for the Pacific Railroad, and they had three sons: Charles, Thomas (Lee's father), and William. Sometime during the 1930s, the family moved to East Los Angeles.

Born in the Wild West, Clara grew into a straight-talking, hardworking, no-nonsense woman. Yet she was kind, loving, and patient. In his grandparents' two-bedroom Boyle Heights home, Lee shared a room with his twenty-four-year-old uncle, William, who was severely mentally disabled. A pound and a half at birth, Lee's uncle would never be able to care for himself, but Clara wouldn't hear any talk of placing him in an institution.

At seven years old, brown-eyed Lee had officially been abandoned by both his parents and now helped his grandmother care for his uncle, who couldn't talk or communicate in any way. Lee helped feed, shave, and bathe William, and on Friday nights, helped his grandmother comb the streets looking for his drunken grandfather. Lee's leg had scarred, but not completely healed. Every time he bent his knee, the skin became uncomfortably taut. But there was no room for self-pity in Clara Baca's house, nor was there in Lee's heart. His uncle was a daily reminder of how good Lee had it, instilling in him an appreciation for life and physical and mental health. Lee learned from Clara's example and came to share her positive outlook, work ethic, and steadfast sense of responsibility. He didn't quite understand what "Put that in your pipe and smoke it" meant, but he knew whatever words his grandmother spoke before the confusing phrase were important and something he should remember. Clara's devotion to both him and his Uncle William deeply impacted Lee. He was grateful for his grandmother's warmth and strength, and he never wanted to disappoint her. And despite his grandfather's struggle with alcohol, he was dutiful in providing for his wife, William, and Lee.

Despite the hardships, those were fond years for Lee. Every Saturday

CHAPTER 1

night the family tuned in to *Hometown Jamboree* on KXLA—"Nothing but Western Music 24 Hours a Day"—and listened to Cliffie Stone's broadcast from the El Monte Legion Stadium. The show introduced Lee to Tennessee Ernie Ford, Johnny Horton, and Ferlin Husky, and fostered a lifetime love of country and Western music. Lee flourished in grammar school, excelling in both English and math and even skipped fourth grade. His classmates were as diverse as the neighborhood and untroubled by each other's race. From them he learned *Leroy* wasn't a typical Mexican name, and that *baka* means *idiot* in Japanese.

Lee made a lifelong friend in Stephen Tuenge, a brainy kid from Minnesota. Stephen taught Lee how to build balsa wood airplanes and kites, which they flew in the park. He also taught Lee how to play chess, Chinese checkers, and the abstract strategy game Go, and he explained the scientific uses of battery power. The boys shared *Little Lulu* comic books and copies of *MAD* magazine. Lee matriculated to Stevenson Middle School, where his classmate—future Los Angeles Dodger Willie Davis—pitched to him in physical education.

During these years, Lee's father came to Tomas and Clara's home for Friday night dinners and gave them money each month for taking care of Lee. The small house had become crowded as Thomas's younger brother, Charles, was also living there while he was out of work. One Friday night, Charles told Thomas he was a lousy father. Impulsively, Thomas told fourteen-year-old Lee, "Get your clothes." Lee fit everything he owned in a cardboard box and the next morning woke up in Cypress Park on the other side of Chavez Ravine.

There was no room for Lee in the tiny one-bedroom apartment Thomas shared with his new wife, but the landlord said the teen could sleep in the building's small utility cellar. The windowless space was lit by a single bare bulb, and with the addition of a metal military cot it became Lee's bedroom. Ever low-maintenance, Lee was grateful for the humble space and the attendant privacy and freedom. Because he spent most of his days and nights in school, working, and socializing—not to mention hours on the bus going from one activity to another—the room was a place to sleep, and that was all Lee needed it to be.

If Lee wanted spending money, he needed to earn it. One of his first jobs was selling newspapers in front of a Safeway market. Other jobs included digging ditches and working at a car wash. Arguably, the worst job he held was one his father helped him get through a connection at the Farmer John slaughterhouse and meatpacking plant. On Saturdays, Lee attended to the pigs that had been railroaded in from Virginia. He'd sweep the hay off the tracks and help place the animals in their stalls. Squealing pigs would rush him at feeding time. As he lifted heavy sacks to pour barley into the troughs, they would press their snouts into his legs and knock him off balance. After taking care of the hogs, he steam-washed the smokehouses. Because the doors had to remain closed, he worked quickly to get out of the humid and noxious enclosures.

Lee, reeking of hog feces, would sit behind the bus driver on the ten-mile trip back to Cypress Park. He noticed the bus driver opened his window whenever he boarded, and Lee hoped it also spared his fellow passengers from his stench.

A people person, Lee was excited to go to Franklin High School, where he'd be able to make new friends. By now, he was taller than most of his classmates. He wanted to play football, but his after-school jobs made it impossible to attend practice. Instead, he joined the track team, where he became a quarter-mile and two-hundred-meter sprinter. He enjoyed traveling to competitions and the camaraderie he shared with like-minded, dedicated athletes. At six-foot-one and 152 pounds, Lee earned varsity letters his junior and senior years.

By always trying to best his personal times and win for his teammates and school, he saw the direct correlation between hard work and success. He joined the Athledelphians, Franklin's athletic club, and was elected senior class president. Because of his position, Lee was able

CHAPTER 1

to enroll in Leadership Class, where he learned about civics and the fundamentals of government. It's hard to imagine in this era of liability lawsuits and school underfunding, but the school district actually owned a Piper Cub airplane, which Lee learned how to fly. Lee wasn't a serious student, but when he heard a presentation by an LAPD officer on Career Day, he was captivated. Suddenly, he knew what he wanted to do with the rest of his life.

Lee graduated high school in 1960. Having spent those years more focused on extracurricular activities than academics, he graduated with a dismal 2.3 GPA. Still, he could proudly say that from first grade through twelfth, he'd never missed a single day of school.

The LAPD had just launched a new cadet program for younger recruits. Eighteen-year-olds could work in non-policing jobs, then enter the academy when they turned twenty-one. All Lee had to do was pass a test. But he failed. And when he told his father on the front porch, Thomas opined, "Well, I didn't think you'd pass anyway." Already heartbroken, Lee went into the backyard and had a good cry. He felt like his life was over. Never had he felt so hopeless. He knew in his heart he could do better, so there was no excuse for not trying his best. He wanted to help people. People like his uncle William. People like his neighbors. The poor. The broken. The addicted. The ones without a voice. Despite the setback at LAPD, he was certain he wanted to work in law enforcement. He needed to do it for his soul. He needed to do it to be the best he could be. Maybe his father's harsh words were the wakeup call he needed.

Lee knew he was capable of passing the LAPD exam, and he wished he had learned how to study in high school. Though his academic track record might indicate otherwise, Lee loved learning. He realized education was the key to a better future. His father and grandparents knew less than he did about college and couldn't offer any advice. So, Lee did what he would continue to do for the rest of his life: He identified the problem and vowed to solve it. He set a goal, figured out what he needed to do, and became tactical. He enrolled at East Los Angeles Community College, which offered a major course of study in police science. Lee had hoped to improve on his high school GPA, but the assortment of part-time jobs that occupied his days and nights still made it difficult. He served ice cream at Baskin-Robbins during the day and worked as a janitor from midnight to five a.m. His demanding work schedule made it impossible to take a full class load. But after four years, he earned his associate's degree in police science.

While working at yet another job—at the Stationers Corporation on Flower Street—Lee fell in love with one of his coworkers, Judith Howell. They married on June 13, 1964, six months after they met. They moved to South Central Los Angeles—to South Gate, which abutted the eastern border of the Watts neighborhood.

A week after their wedding, Lee left for boot camp at Marine Corps Base Camp Pendleton. Fit from his running regimen and confidant that he could achieve anything he set his mind to, Lee endured thirteen weeks of physical, psychological, and emotional challenges, written exams, and the dreaded Crucible. He was meritoriously promoted to Private First Class. Graduates had the option of going into active duty or joining the Reserves. Lee chose the latter.

Now twenty-three, Lee found a job closer to home and worked in the tool crib at Monogram Precision Industry, Inc., which made ovens for airplanes. The job paid the rent, but Lee needed to be challenged. He was planning his next move when one of his coworkers, Melvin Block, suggested he join the Los Angeles Sheriff's Department. His younger brother, Sherman, was a sergeant in their vice bureau and apparently loved working there. Despite failing the LAPD test six years earlier, Lee hadn't given up on his dream to work in law enforcement. He and Judith wanted to start a family, and sheriff's deputies made a good living. The job would be mentally and physically stimulating, and above all, he'd be able to help and protect people.

Chapter 2

The Grinder

"I've never been someone to think that I'm the greatest at anything, but I'm a very strong-willed individual who believes in constant creativity and constant growth."

With the minimum required score, Lee barely passed the rigorous LASD entrance examination. As a member of Class 108, he began his training at the sheriff's academy at Biscailuz Training Center in Monterey Park in the spring of 1965.

Dressed in a suit and tie, briefcase in hand, Lee arrived early for his first day of training filled with excitement and an equal sense of composure. His eyes took in every detail of the sprawling hillside campus. A mix of Southern California scrub, dirt, green grass, and low-slung buildings, the grounds included a firing range, rows of black-and-white patrol cars, and tan- and green-clad deputies in friendly conversation. His heart swelled with promise. The world felt right. For his whole life, Lee had moved from house to house and job to job. The feeling that he had now found his home was powerful and certain. He and the other recruits were given a warm welcome, which included a tour of the campus and an overview of how they would be spending the next thirteen weeks. That was the first day.

But the sheriff's academy was designed to be physically and psychologically brutal. The thinking was that anyone who could weather the stress, abuse, and relentless demands could survive the mean streets of Los Angeles County. The inculcation began the minute the young recruits lined up to check in on their second day, and it didn't let up until those who had the fortitude to last until the end completed the program. Though the uniforms were different, the training officers at Biscailuz Center reminded Lee of the drill sergeants he had faced two years earlier. Already a Marine, Lee was confident he had the mettle to withstand anything the instructors threw his way. Nothing rattled him: the uniform inspections, spit-flying-in-your-face rebukes, and seemingly endless formation marches across the legendary "grinder," the asphalt slab where the worst of the humiliation and physical training took place. Lee knew the pain was only temporary; he would hang tough.

At the academy, recruits were divided into platoons and rotated through different training exercises and classes. Each recruit needed to model everything the department stood for. As sheriff's deputies, any one of them could be a citizen's only encounter with law enforcement. One ill-chosen harsh word or violation of policy out in the field could erode the public's trust in the department and undermine years of good work.

The LASD constantly updated its *Manual of Policy and Procedures* based on real-life events. Class 108 was taught department regulations, the application of various laws, radio codes, and how to write a report. They practiced tactical restraint techniques, baton usage, as well as first aid and radio operations. The training officers at the firing range demonstrated hands-on weapon safety and marksmanship.

CHAPTER 2

Some instruction was scenario-based and involved role-playing, such as search and arrest techniques.

Though the days were indeed long—and hot—Lee found they went by too quickly. He didn't find the training as exhausting as his classmates. Invigorated, he was usually one of the last of his class to leave campus and the first to arrive in the morning. Driven and hungry to learn as much as he could, Lee created study habits that had eluded him in high school. He'd always thrived on little sleep, so at home and under the quiet of night, he would review the day's lessons, memorize laws and codes, and replay tactical techniques.

As Lee embarked on his career and life with his new bride, there was an eddy building in the city. It would be a summer Los Angeles would never forget. And for the second time in his twenty-three years, racial riots would come within a couple miles of Lee Baca's home.

Driving his mother's 1955 Buick, twenty-one-year-old Marquette Frye was two blocks from his home in Watts, California, when he was pulled over by a state highway patrol motorcycle officer for suspicion of driving under the influence. It was August 11, 1965. Marquette was on parole for robbery, so while the officer began field sobriety tests, his passenger—brother Ronald—ran home to get their mother.

Marquette joked with the officer, saying that though it appeared he had been weaving his car, he had just been dodging potholes. As they both laughed, onlookers gathered to watch the exchange. For nearby residents, the sight of a white police officer questioning a young Black man was commonplace, but all too often escalated to verbal and physical abuse. The tension between the neighborhood's mostly Black population and law enforcement had long been teetering on a critical precipice. What happened next would catapult Watts to infamy and come to represent the extent of the acrimony between people of color and the police on a national level.

SHERIFF LEE BACA

In America's Second Great Migration, which lasted from 1940 to 1970, millions of Black Americans—tormented by the Jim Crow South's institutionalized economic, social, and educational racism, not to mention the ritual unprovoked harassment, beatings, and lynchings—uprooted in search of a better life. In the first Great Migration (1916–1940) from the South, the exodus had been predominantly to the North and Midwest. This time, migrants headed west. In signing Executive Order 8802 in 1941, President Franklin Roosevelt had prohibited discrimination in the defense industry, which was ramping up production for the war effort. With so many Anglo boys enlisting in the military, there was a shortage of workers in the factories. Southern California alone was home to 60 to 70 percent of the burgeoning aerospace industry, including Douglas Aircraft, Lockheed, Northrop, Hughes Aircraft, and McDonnell Aircraft.

Enticed by the economic possibilities and hopeful racial discrimination would be restrained by the physical borders they were crossing, thousands of Black families moved to the region. They would come to find that although Los Angeles didn't have de jure segregation, exclusive housing covenants limited where people of color could settle. Homeowners in predominantly white neighborhoods were legally prohibited from selling their houses to any person of color, nor would landlords rent to them. The Home Owners' Loan Corporation, which the government had sponsored to make it easier for Americans to buy houses, had published color-coded maps of US cities that identified neighborhood ethnic composition and desirability. In Los Angeles, Beverly Hills was green, meaning it was virtually a "whites only" town. East Los Angeles and South Central Los Angeles were red. For those who lived in one of the redlined areas—as they came to be called—it was all but impossible to get any kind of loan from a bank. As more people of color moved to the county, neighborhoods became clearly defined by race creating a sober legacy that remains to this day.

CHAPTER 2

Once dubbed the "white spot of America," the city of Los Angeles was home to approximately 63,700 Black residents in 1940. By 1965, that number had astonishingly boomed to 350,000. And despite the vast swaths of undeveloped land and available housing, these newcomers were confined to live in redlined neighborhoods that comprised 40 square miles out of Los Angeles County's 4,700.

In 1963, Martin Luther King Jr. delivered his "I Have a Dream" speech at the March on Washington. That same year, the California legislature passed the Rumford Fair Housing Act, which affirmed "the practice of discrimination because of race, color, religion, national origin, or ancestry in housing accommodations is declared to be against public policy." The following year, the US government passed the Civil Rights Act, putting an end to segregation and discrimination.

In response, the California Real Estate Association fought back: "Millions of homeowners of the Caucasian race have constructed or acquired homes in areas restricted against occupancy by Negroes. The practice of surrounding homes in such areas with the security of such restrictions has become a traditional element of value in homeownership throughout this nation." Their statement went on to say: "The threat of occupancy by Negroes of property in such areas depreciates the value of all home properties and constitutes a direct deterrent to investment in the construction or acquisition of homes of superior quality whether large or small. The experience has been uniform that whenever and wherever Negroes have occupied homes in such areas this has not only depreciated values of the properties which they own but has depreciated the values of all surrounding properties." Shamefully, over 65 percent of California voters agreed with the sentiment and voted yes on Proposition 14, which overturned the Rumford Fair Housing Act until a 1967 US Supreme Court ruling.

Just twelve miles from the Pacific Ocean, Watts had been on a seemingly endless downward spiral. It was the most densely populated area in the US. Its schools performed among the worst in the county, and several elementary schools didn't even have cafeterias. Two-thirds of high school students never graduated. Denied the opportunities available to other Angelenos, conditions and consequences of poverty fueled the growing despair. Like the rest of the nation, Watts had lost loved ones in the Vietnam War. The surviving soldiers who had served their country with honor returned to a town in worse condition than when they had left. Jobs were scarce, and their parents—housekeepers, nannies, and butlers—spoke of lush estates and unimagined wealth. Reminded of stories their grandparents had told of plantation life, it seemed like nothing had changed—they were still relegated to the "little house" in a seemingly endless spiral of failure. The ongoing harassment and violence Watts's Black residents and their families endured at the hands of police became a tangible representation of everything that was wrong in their lives.

Ever since the mayor of Los Angeles had appointed him chief of the LAPD in 1950, William Parker had been on a mission to clean up the department renowned for its corruption. He had served as an army captain in World War II and earned a Purple Heart after being wounded in the Normandy invasion. His experiences in the military influenced how he would run his police department. He managed to turn the roughshod organization into a professional force that became the national paradigm.

Parker's approach to law enforcement was hardcore. With unambiguous racism, he stated, "It is estimated that by 1970, 45 percent of the metropolitan area of Los Angeles will be Negro . . . If you want any protection for your home and family . . . you're going to have to get in and support a strong police department." Of Latinos, he explained, lawlessness was due to "being too far removed from the wild tribes of the inner mountains of Mexico." Parker's mostly white LAPD recruits came from the South and/or had just come off tours with the marine corps and army. His department was segregated. White and Black officers never shared patrol cars.

When Parker put a stop to foot patrol in certain neighborhoods, any chance of officers developing relationships with citizens in communities such as Watts were lost. Ensconced in their slow-rolling black-and-white Plymouth Savoys—trawling the streets of South Central Los Angeles—police became further dehumanized and severed from the community. When Parker scrubbed an outreach program that serviced disenfranchised youth through summer camps, picnics, and other activities, he effectively ended any hope of building bridges between the LAPD and communities of color.

Black citizens were harassed by the LAPD just for being on the "wrong" side of town, and their complaints of police brutality—including racial slurs, abuse, and unprovoked violence and questioning—went ignored by the department. Terms such as "justifiable homicide" had become a chilling part of the vernacular when describing fatalities at the hands of officers. Without the means to retain lawyers and take their grievances to the courts the victims had no voice. With no trust in the system, their animosity toward the police festered like an open wound.

In the 1960s, the entire country was under strain. Anxiety over the Cold War, Bay of Pigs, Kennedy assassination, and Vietnam War was demoralizing. In protests on college campuses and along Main Street, a growing antiestablishment counterculture challenged institutional thinking and demanded justice. No matter how peaceful the protestors' intentions or whether their cause be anti-war, anti-nukes, or pro–Equal Rights Amendment and Civil Rights, cities called in police to maintain peace and order. The largely Caucasian forces symbolized the strong arm of the government and everything the protestors were against. Battling chaos and organized radical groups such as the Black Panthers and Students for a Democratic Society (SDS), and pelted by rocks and bricks and profane insults, law enforcement officers not only felt under attack, they *were* under attack.

It was in this social context, while Lee Baca finished his training at the sheriff's academy, that a routine traffic stop escalated into one of the most explosive events in the history of Los Angeles.

Marquette Frye failed his sobriety test. Accounts differ on the details of exactly what happened when, though the consensus is that by the time his brother returned with their mother, Rena Price, the initial levity of the traffic stop had deteriorated to anything but. A couple of dozen spectators had gathered to watch as Marquette resisted arrest and the officer radioed for backup. By the time another motorcycle patrolman and a patrol car arrived, the crowd had grown to a few hundred. When Rena saw how roughly her son was being handled, she jumped on an officer's back. In the scrum that followed, Marquette was struck on the forehead with a baton.

Twenty-three minutes after the traffic stop, Marquette, his brother, and their mother were under arrest. Remarkably, the number of onlookers had reached a thousand. When one spat at a couple officers as they were leaving, they breached the mob to arrest the woman. Mistakingly believing she was pregnant, the churning mob surrounded the officers as they dragged her away. The crowd came unglued, reason blinded by the pain and frustration bottled inside for so long, now erupting in an unchecked release.

More police arrived brandishing batons and shotguns. The crowd pelted them with rocks, bottles, and bricks. The violence continued unabated and began to spread to other streets. White motorists stuck in the consequent traffic jam were pulled out of their cars and beaten. Buildings and cars were set on fire. Stores were looted. Snipers fired at police and firefighters.

The governor called in 14,000 National Guard troops and imposed an eight p.m. curfew on the affected area which had grown

CHAPTER 2

to encompass nearly fifty square miles. Six days after the traffic stop, peace was finally restored. Those who were there described it as a war zone. When the Watts Riots—now sometimes referenced as the Watts Rebellion—finally ended, the statistics told a sorry story: thirty-four Black citizens killed, three first responders killed, 1,032 injured, 3,952 arrested, and over $40 million in property damage. It is estimated that about 15 percent of the area's residents participated in the riots.

That same month, Lee Baca graduated in the top five of his class and was sworn in as a deputy of the Los Angeles County Sheriff's Department.

Chapter 3

The Starting Line

"I finally got to the place where I could do something that was really overwhelmingly powerful from a career point of view, and it was all based on the transformation of mediocrity, because I didn't want to be viewed as a mediocre performer."

Even lifelong native Angelenos can be hard-pressed to understand the differences and division of responsibilities between the Los Angeles Police Department and the Los Angeles County Sheriff's Department. Each was founded in the same era—LASD in 1850, LAPD in 1869—but differs in its command structure and jurisdiction. The chief of police is appointed by the Los Angeles City Council and reports to a police commission. The sheriff is elected to a four-year term by the constituents, and though funded by the Los Angeles County Board of Supervisors, doesn't answer to them. The sheriff's powers are defined by the California Constitution.

SHERIFF LEE BACA

The LAPD and LASD serve different geographic communities, though there are some confusing overlaps. Simply put, the LASD is the law enforcement agency for the *county* of Los Angeles, and the LAPD for the *city* of Los Angeles.

Los Angeles County covers over 4,700 square miles—about the size of Delaware and Rhode Island combined. The city of Los Angeles is the seat of Los Angeles County and one of eighty-eight incorporated cities within it, which include Burbank, Calabasas, Compton, Inglewood, Long Beach, Malibu, Pasadena, etc. Some of these cities have their own police departments, but almost half have a contract with the LASD. The sheriff's department even has jurisdiction of Santa Catalina Island, twenty-five miles off the coastline. Over ten million people live in Los Angeles County, four million of them in the city of Los Angeles. Each year, sheriff's deputies arrest more than ninety thousand felony and misdemeanor suspects and respond to over a million service calls.

The city of Los Angeles is approximately five hundred square miles and encompasses familiar communities that sound like they *should* be cities, such as Venice, Boyle Heights, Hollywood, Van Nuys, Watts, and Bel Air. But none of these are actually independent cities. They're all part of the socially, ethnically, and economically diverse quilt that is the city of Los Angeles. Some squares are missing from the quilt—separate cities such as Beverly Hills, Santa Monica, and West Hollywood. An LAPD patrol car driving the eleven miles from Bel-Air to Hollywood passes through two other police jurisdictions on the way: the Beverly Hills Police Department and the Los Angeles County Sheriff's Department, which has a contract with the city of West Hollywood.

To make matters even more complex, the LASD now provides policing and security services for the county's Metropolitan Transit Authority, which includes the buses, trains, and subways that traverse the *city* of Los Angeles, LAPD territory. And in 2001, the LASD merged with the Los Angeles Community College Police Department,

CHAPTER 3

meaning the LAPD might police the roads that surround a college, but once you drive onto campus, you're in sheriff's country.

The Los Angeles Sheriff's Department has four divisions: patrol, custody, court services, and administration. But when Lee Baca graduated from the academy, the department had only two: patrol and custody.

The custody division, where all new deputies are first assigned, oversees the county's jails. The virtue of this rite of passage continues to be analyzed and debated. Advocates argue that placing green trainees in a controlled, gun-free environment is more prudent than sending them out to patrol unpredictable streets with a Smith & Wesson strapped to their side. It is during their custody rotation that most trainees first encounter the ilk of criminals they'll face on the street (in an *uncontrolled* environment)—miscreants who wouldn't hesitate to put a bullet in the head of anyone wearing a badge or would do so *because* of their badge. In the jails, trainees become familiar with the bone-chilling "felon stare," gang language and culture, and the criminal mind, all to better prepare them for patrol.

Though intended to last six to twelve months, trainees' custody assignments have historically stretched far beyond, sometimes for as long as five or six years. The reason? Perennial budget cuts that lead to hiring freezes, suspending the influx of new trainees from the academy. With no one to replace them, deputies stay in custody until the academy reopens and hiring restarts.

Opponents of sending new graduates to the jails for their first assignment assert that exposing these impressionable young men and women to the worst of society—especially for so long—has an adverse effect. They contend that when deputies begin their first patrol assignment, many have already become hardened and cynical. And though they attend a short patrol school, their academy training is by then too far in the past.

SHERIFF LEE BACA

Freshly minted from the academy, Lee was assigned to Wayside Honor Rancho (now Pitchess Detention Center) in Castaic. His commute from South Gate was one hundred miles roundtrip.

Established by Sheriff Eugene Biscailuz in 1938, Wayside Honor Rancho housed men awaiting trial, sentencing, and transportation to state prison. The three thousand–acre pastoral facility in the northern reaches of L.A. County defies conventional ideas of what a jail looks like. Over the years, the facility has added maximum-security divisions, but Wayside started out as a minimum-security prison. There, inmates needing nominal supervision paid their dues to society by maintaining a profitable and virtually self-sustaining farm. Inmates tended the 250 acres of alfalfa and hay needed to care for the herds of sheep and cattle that roamed the surrounding hills. These animals, along with seven hundred–plus head of hogs, provided milk and meat needed by Wayside inmates as well as those in other county facilities. The orchards, vegetable gardens, and bakery rounded out their diet. Prisoners also handcrafted items such as wooden toys, which were donated to hospitals and other charities or sold to visitors.

Wayside may already seem like a utopian ideal of what criminal rehabilitation could be. But sometimes the Golden State offers up a little unexpected extra magic. In 1951, oil was discovered on the property. Five years later, the property's thirty-one wells added an estimated $750,000 a year to the county's general fund.

Lee was assigned to Wayside's maximum-security section. His duties included roll call counts, bunk inspections, letting wards in and out of their cells, and managing the desk. From day one, he saw each inmate as a human being deserving of his respect: folks who had lost their way through unfortunate circumstances and poor choices. Lee listened to their life stories and the challenges they faced.

In 1965, the department wasn't faced with the budget crises of today, so Lee's assignment to custody ended as scheduled. On

CHAPTER 3

August 23, 1965, Lee Baca was sworn in as a sheriff's deputy by Sheriff Peter J. Pitchess.

Lee was sent to the department's oldest station, East Los Angeles, for his patrol training. The seven-and-a-half-square-mile area he patrolled was home. He knew the streets. He knew the culture and many of the faces. He worked the heavy crime shift—midnight to eight a.m.—and he and his partner specialized in catching burglars in the act of breaking into closed businesses. A rookie, Lee was already deeply troubled by how some of his fellow deputies abused the power of the badge. While some of his peers followed the "hook and book" model in hopes of building up their arrest records, Lee preferred employing reason and compassion. He favored having conversations with offenders, leaving them with a warning and something to think about. The way he saw it, helping transgressors change their ways would have more of an enduring impact than ineffective punishment

After patrol, he was reassigned to the recruitment division. Handsome, friendly, and always looking crisp in his uniform, Lee was the ideal representative for the department. Lee completed his training with a posting back at the academy.

Twenty-four years old in 1966, Lee became a father. Judith blessed him with twins—a boy and a girl. The following year, the couple bought their first home. The monthly payment on their $23,500 bungalow near the Santa Anita Racetrack in Arcadia was $105. Proud of his son's accomplishment, Lee's father came over on Lee's days off to help him paint it.

After earning his sergeant's stripes in 1968, Lee was assigned to Temple City Station—conveniently, the closest to his new home. Interested in education as a form of outreach, he earned a K–12 teaching credential from UCLA, and after transferring to the Sheriff's Community Relations Office, enlisted the help of Richard Weintraub from the Constitutional Rights Foundation in developing an LASD pilot program for junior high and high school students. "Student and the Law" provided teens with an understanding of the lawmaking process and administration of justice, covering a range of topics from delinquency to drugs. Lee was the program's first instructor and developed a comfortable rapport with his students.

After the pilot program's success, Lee and Weintraub worked to bring the course to more schools throughout Los Angeles County and trained other officers to teach the class. Over the next seven years, Lee taught at Faye Ross Middle School, Garfield Adult School, and Carson High School. There was no other curriculum like it in the country. As word spread, it became a national model.

The program's benefits were multifold. As a stopgap, the after-school and weekend activities kept children and teens from getting into trouble, even if only for a few hours—and hopefully they'd have fun and learn something as well. But for too many inner-city kids, sheriffs were the ever-changing (and mostly white) faces that looked them up and down from their patrol cars, frisked their neighbors on the sidewalk, and harassed their older brothers and fathers. Just by getting out of their black-and-whites and uniforms, deputies became real people, not merely blank faces representing a begrudged institution. Likewise, deputies came to know members of the community and appreciate their day-to-day concerns and struggles. The class helped build bridges between the department and community.

Sometimes playing the role of the arresting officer in reenactments, Lee also participated in criminal justice seminars for high school students. In addition to his work in secondary schools, Lee joined the faculty at Cerritos College, teaching "Rules of Evidence" and "Police Community Relations."

Though already a teacher, Lee became a student again. A true believer in the transformative power of education, he enrolled at California State University at Los Angeles to study justice administration.

CHAPTER 3

Coincidentally, while there, Lee met the man who had unknowingly set the course for his life. His former coworker's brother, Sherman Block—the LASD sergeant (now captain) who loved his job—was his classmate. Block would later become the first deputy to work his way through all the ranks in the chain of command before becoming sheriff in 1982. He became Lee's mentor and lifelong friend.

Lee earned his bachelor of science in 1971 and made the dean's list all four quarters.

After their initial assignment to custody, it is unusual for sworn personnel to spend an extended amount of time at any one station or in any one position. Depending on the needs of the various divisions, units, and stations, as well as vacancies left by retiring or promoted deputies, the staff is always in flux. Some positions are more coveted than others, and though placement is never guaranteed, officers can put in a request for assignments. Many want to work at stations closer to home or at those that are slower. Some ask for the easiest jobs or the ones that help get them promoted sooner. But throughout his career, it was Lee's habit to apply for the least desirable, most difficult.

After his promotion to lieutenant in 1971, Lee served in the Central, South, and East Patrol Divisions at four different stations: East Los Angeles (1971–1973), Altadena (1973–1974), Carson (1974–1976), and Lennox (now South Los Angeles, 1976–1978). His self-stated mission was: "To serve the public, the department, and my captain and subordinates with leadership and management that is open, creative, fair, consistent, accountable, and reliable. To practice what I preach."

A station's lieutenant, who reports to the captain, supervises deputies and sergeants. In his new position, Lee directed and commanded high-risk field activities, such as responses to armed robberies, crimes in progress, and officer-involved shootings. He also oversaw patrol and scheduled assignments, conducted training briefings, approved arrests, and evaluated subordinates' job performance, recommending disciplinary measures to his captain when necessary.

As he rose through the organization, Lee became acutely aware of its problems. It was a complex bureaucracy where changes were slow to execute. Failures in policy and training were revealed under both routine and unique circumstances at the station level from those with front-row seats. But it took individuals' tenacity for proposed revisions to reach the right people to propel the information upstream.

Many of the problems that create the highest risk for police and the public are when seemingly minor and routine situations, such as traffic stops or noise complaints, escalate rapidly. An inveterate trait of Lee's is that he likes to solve problems. And large, noisy parties had been presenting a lot of problems leading to unnecessary use of force. The issue wasn't new, but Lee felt a new approach was needed. One time was too many for a simple one a.m. nuisance complaint from a tired and disgruntled neighbor to conclude with fired weapons and an injured or dead victim.

Lee began studying the issue from all angles. He drew on his own experiences responding to large party calls and talked to other officers and deputies about theirs. This being the pre-computer age, there was no searchable database to easily find relevant incident reports. Lee needed to cull the station's file cabinets, folder by folder. Each event he analyzed read like the last. Responding to a complaint, two deputies would soon find themselves outnumbered by youth emboldened by liquor and their cheering friends. It only took one knucklehead to mouth off and one deputy to overreact. After a tirade of insults and threats, a shoving match would ensue with no one really sure who shoved who first. One bystander would step in. Then another. Feeling things were quickly getting out of control, a deputy would draw his weapon in impatience or panic. It was textbook.

Seeing that the scenario was predictable and avoidable, Lee penned a department publication called "Policing Large Parties." Part of his

CHAPTER 3

solution was that officers anticipate the problem and have an executable plan in place to prevent it from getting out of hand in the first place. Unless dealing with someone strung out on drugs or mentally ill, Lee found that many situations could be diffused with sincere respect and tactical communication—words that expressed understanding and elicited the other person's better self. It was a brave stance to take in a paramilitary organization, and many scoffed at Lee's progressive ideas. But the importance of thoughtful communication would become a theme throughout Lee's career, as would his progressive approach to solving problems.

Lee continued teaching and speaking at community events, groups, and clubs. He was approachable with a natural confidence and ease whether behind the microphone or in a one-on-one conversation. While he cultivated these skills, he grew as a leader and manager.

When Lee wasn't working or with his family, he was back in the classroom, this time in the master of public administration program at the University of Southern California. Though the campus was just a few miles from where Lee grew up, the idea of attending USC would have been unimaginable in his youth. Lee was humbled and filled with gratitude as he passed the Romanesque red brick edifices. Now a Trojan, he bled cardinal and gold and, when he managed to get a ticket, went to every football game he could. When he could get two, he'd bring his father. He earned his master's degree in 1973 with a 4.0 grade point average, a far cry from the 2.3 he carried in high school.

After his posting at Lennox Station, Lee moved to the Advocate's Office, which represented the department in disciplinary hearings before the Civil Service Commission, where sworn personnel were disciplined for violating policy and unethical behavior both on- and off-duty. (Criminal misconduct was handled through different channels and the decision to prosecute was up the district attorney.) The most common hearings were disputes about discipline for preventable traffic collisions, skipping mandatory training, and performing below department standards. More serious infractions included negligently handling prisoners, constitutional violations, excessive use of force, sexual harassment, and endangering other officers. Deputies and officers were also disciplined for spousal battery, drunk driving, and misuse of their position or authority. In or out of uniform, each employee had to bring honor to the department. The public's trust depended on it.

Station captains followed recommended guidelines for appropriate discipline. Sometimes training, counseling, and a performance review period were mandated. More serious offenses could result in discharge from duty and suspension without pay for up to thirty days. Deputies had the right to appeal proposed sanctions, and when they did, they pled their cases to the Civil Service Commission. The deputies had nothing to lose and everything to gain by trying to overturn or reduce their punishments. The Association for Los Angeles Deputy Sheriffs (ALADS) union had lawyers at the ready, and to the department's great frustration (as well as the public's), the Civil Service Commission overturned department-imposed discipline more often than not.

The department was at a perennial disadvantage as budgetary restraints inhibited it from hiring lawyers to defend its sanctions. So, officers such as Lee acted as paralegals and argued against attorneys who specialized in civil service hearings. In Lee's three years with the unit, he advocated over 180 hearings, prevailing in 177. In one of the three he lost, the appellant's attorney was Stephen Reinhardt, whom President Jimmy Carter later appointed as a judge on the US Court of Appeals for the Ninth Circuit.

It was around this time—at thirty-six years old—that Lee became a self-described fitness nut. He'd hit the track at 5:30 a.m., rain or shine, in a precise and strictly disciplined ritual. His daily eight miles started off at an easy pace until he went all out at the end. He timed and

CHAPTER 3

recorded each run, always trying to beat his personal best. He would run twelve quarter-miles and take a recovery lap before going again. One day a week he warmed up on the track, then broke into a full-speed uphill sprint. He ended each workout with 400 crunches and 360 push-ups.

Lee was a regular participant in charity 10Ks and in the annual 120-mile Challenge Cup Baker-to-Vegas Relay Race in which over two hundred teams from law enforcement agencies around the country compete.

His practice was inviolable. Once while his traveling companions collapsed on their hotel beds after traveling eighteen hours to Pakistan on a counterterrorism sortie in 2004, Lee hit the track. Guards from the elite Pakistani police had trouble keeping up with his seven-minute-mile pace around the Lahore polo field.

In a 2007 interview with *Runner's World*, Lee stated:

> Running is a method of keeping your body in a state of preparedness, and that preparedness obviously feeds your mind. . . . You have to put on a suit of armor, and fitness is that suit of armor as far as I'm concerned. . . . If I can do intervals that are excruciatingly difficult in preparation for competitive racing, then I can pretty much put up with anything. . . . Running teaches you to be very, very tough on yourself and then that toughness translates into dealing with problems in a more calm way.

The article ended with this quote from Lee: "Your body is your house. You owe it to yourself to arrange it in the best way possible. And if you don't, no one will do it for you. You can create a palace in yourself or the world will be your jail."

Chapter 4

Two Gold Bars

"The badge does not make the person. The person makes the badge."

Sheriff Pitchess pinned Lee with his captain's bars in 1981. In October of that year, Lee moved into his new office in the city of Norwalk, one of the department's forty contract cities. Rather than training and managing their own police forces, smaller municipalities' resources were better spent and their citizens better served by contracting with what many considered to be the best sheriff's department in the country. Through their partnership with LASD, the municipalities had access to services they could never fund on their own. The LASD's aero bureau, canine unit, special enforcement bureau, and crime lab were among the nation's best, outfitted with the latest technology and staffed by highly skilled specialists.

Collaborating with mayors and city councils, local captains provided services tailored to each municipality's needs and budgets. They drafted service plans to address crime trends particular to each city, working out tough decisions and compromises as to how many deputies and patrol cars would serve the constituents. City budgets were stretched thin, and without fail their managers wanted—and needed—more than they could afford. At the same time, it was imperative that captains were certain they could provide the high-quality service for which the department was known. Misjudgments could have grave consequences for the community, plus expose the department to unnecessary liability and harm its reputation.

Norwalk Station was the command post for multiple contract cities at the county's southeasternmost reaches. For the next five years, Lee managed 260 personnel and a $12 million budget to police and protect the region's two hundred thousand citizens. In servicing a contract city, a station captain assumes a role not unlike that of a local chief of police. (Consider that ninety percent of the police departments in the US have fewer than fifty officers and almost half have fewer than ten.)

Captains are encouraged to run their stations as they see fit and have the latitude to create a culture that aligns with their management style, as long as it adheres to the department's standards, core values, and budget.

Upon his arrival at Norwalk, Captain Baca set three goals—goals that would become thematic throughout his career:

1. Broaden the station's roles in community relations and education.
2. Improve communication within the station.
3. Improve crime-fighting and better utilize the station's resources.

Frustrated by the department's tendency to address problems with policy or training after an incident rather than prophylactically, Lee was excited for the chance to implement some of the ideas he had been formulating. More broadly, he believed law enforcement needed critical reform and innovation.

CHAPTER 4

During the seventeenth and eighteenth centuries in the United States, policing was informal and inconsistent. Town constables supervised night watch shifts, which were carried out by well-intended citizens or by scofflaws as part of their sentencing. Some clung to the power that had been handed to them, consequently harassing and bullying the public. Others simply got drunk and slept through their shifts.

As cities and crime grew hand in hand, so did the need for better policing. After a surge of workers' protests and strikes led to riots, local merchants and factory owners sought to control their workers and quash their sometimes violent insubordination. In response, the US's first professional police department was established in Boston in 1838. By the end of the century, most major cities followed suit including both Los Angeles city and county.

These new police departments were staffed by men with no training who actually paid local politicians for their jobs and promotions. After buying entrée into the department, new policemen were handed a badge and a billy club and sent to the streets. There was no oversight or accountability, and corruption was rampant. Tavern owners, gambling dens, and politicians routinely paid cops to look the other way. Police corruption at the turn of the nineteenth century was rampant. From the days of Tammany Hall through Prohibition, police were part of the web of corruption between politicians and organized crime, facilitating election fraud, racketeering, gambling, and prostitution. Bribery and use of excessive force went unchecked in what is dubbed the "political era" of policing.

In the days of the night watchmen, policing had been mostly reactionary, triggered by a specific criminal act. With the advent of organized departments, the focus shifted to preventative crime control, which created problems of its own. Preventing crime requires information and intuition, which come with experience and historical data. Where and when are crimes most likely to occur? In looking for patterns based on their own experiences, police began drawing profiles about who was most likely to break the law. In focusing on maintaining public order and breaking up strikes, police came to categorize the poor, immigrants, and free Black people in the North as "dangerous classes." Preventative crime control gave the police permission to surveil and question citizens at will, thereby creating a breeding ground for unchecked discrimination and harassment.

Concerned about the nation's rising crime rate and accusations of police incompetence, President Hoover formed the Wickersham Commission in 1929. August Vollmer, the former police chief of Berkeley, California, helped write the commission's report. The reforms Vollmer had instituted in Berkeley to separate police from political influence had made its police department the paradigm of everything a modern, successful agency could be. Vollmer is considered the "father of modern policing," and a century later, many of his ideas are still in play.

Vollmer introduced the idea of "professional policing" and advocated for a commitment to impartially enforce the law. He founded the country's first training academy, mandated that his officers get college degrees, and carefully screened all recruits. By offering attractive salaries, he established that policing could be a lasting and legitimate career. Having served in the Spanish–American War, Vollmer introduced a chain of command similar to the military's. He also created a criminal records and crime statistics system to share with other police agencies. And despite public ridicule, he introduced bicycles, and later motorcycles and cars, to effectuate more efficient patrol. Under Vollmer, Berkeley police were among the first to experiment with new technologies, including radio communication, the lie detector, fingerprint classification, handwriting analysis, and forensics. Vollmer believed it important that police cultivate a relationship with the community and citizens they serve, and work with juveniles as the first step in crime prevention. His innovations became standard in this new era of policing. Vollmer's positions took deeper root in 1943 when a book by his former student O. W. Wilson titled *Police Administration* became the bible for the industry. Corruption declined under the professional policing model, but abuses of authority continued, deepening the divide between law enforcement and people of color, immigrants, and the poor.

With the Civil Rights Movement and Vietnam War in the 1960s and 1970s, the relationship between the public and the police became fragile, tense, and violent. In one decade, the national crime rate doubled. The federal government formed the Law Enforcement Assistance Administration in 1968, paving the way for the militarization of police. Departments used the influx of funds to purchase riot gear, armored vehicles, advanced weaponry, helicopters, and other new technologies that had been developed for the Vietnam and Cold Wars. In response to the Watts Riots, the LAPD established a paramilitary Special Weapons and Tactics (SWAT) team to manage future urban unrest and rioting. Other cities formed similar units.

From 1960 to 1985, serious crime in the United States had risen threefold and was projected to keep climbing. Studies consistently concluded what was already evident: current policing strategies were ineffective, and things were only going to get worse. A new "community policing" approach was generating interest as a way to improve public-police relations and reduce crime. Departments began hiring more people of color and women and adopted a "satisfied customer" mentality. Officers were encouraged to make every interaction with the public a positive and personal experience.

From Lee's first days in the academy, it was clear to his training officers and fellow trainees that he was different. When he was around, the most mundane discussions quickly turned philosophical, leaving many of his peers perplexed and struggling to catch up to the cerebral shift in the conversation. Lee seemed to perceive ideas at a higher octave and would cut through to the heart and soul of an issue from a spiritual and humanistic point of view. If there was a typical personality profile for a sheriff's deputy, Lee wasn't it. At times he felt like an outsider, but it didn't bother him. Gentle and centered, he could play hardball when needed. Despite his nonconformity—or perhaps because of it—Lee was respected by his superiors as well as those he led.

His earnestness and genuine concern for people were unmistakable. He treated everyone, no matter their walk in life, with respect. Community leaders liked working with him and citizens felt heard by him. He was always looking for ways to improve the department and to creatively address problems in operations. Plus, he had ideas—a vision of what the department could be, of what Los Angeles could be.

Lee had been an early believer in community-oriented policing, long before it was even a term. It resonated with his personal philosophy, deep respect for life, and concern for others. In one of his favorite books, *The Denial of Death*, author Ernest Becker wrote, "The crisis of modern society is precisely that the youth no longer feel heroic in the plan for action that their culture has set up. They don't believe it is empirically true to the problems of their lives and times." Lee was certain of the power of love, respect, and education in guiding youth to their full potential.

In 1968, Harvard University Press published James Q. Wilson's *Varieties of Police Behavior: The Management of Law and Order in Eight Communities*, which would become one of the most influential studies of law enforcement. Wilson classified policing styles into three categories: watchman, legalistic, and service. In a watchman approach, the goal is to keep the peace, but at the patrolman's discretion. An example would be issuing a verbal warning rather than a citation. In legalistic departments, every officer follows the strict letter of the law, leading to more arrests and citations. Service-oriented departments are attentive to the community's needs and make judgments on a case-by-case basis.

When asked by the *Los Angeles Times* in 1997 to define community

CHAPTER 4

policing, Lee answered, "Community-based policing, in its simplest definition, is creating a partnership with individuals in a given community." In the same article, he stated, "Arrests are [sic] very important part of what a policeman has to do. However, preventing juveniles and adults from committing crimes is just as important."

The sworn personnel at Norwalk knew the station was in for some big changes when their new captain asked them to write a vision statement. Mystified and none too thrilled with the assignment, they submitted a few suggestions, of which Lee chose the strongest: "At Norwalk Station we have one and only one ambition: To be the best. What else is there?"

Lee immediately and unilaterally tackled the goals he had set. "I wanted to solve problems, not be caught by them," he later said.

As captain, he kept his finger on the pulse of each community. He'd never needed much sleep and was well accustomed to thirteen-hour workdays. Local community groups, businesses, and politicians knew Lee would be at their meetings, functions, and fundraisers, day or night. Never wanting to disappoint, Lee routinely attended back-to-back events during his lengthy career.

Lee had always regarded life as a gift. He believed people are inherently good but can be corrupted by hopelessness. In too many homes, crime had become the family business. Too many children were joining gangs. Too many people were addicted to drugs. Too many were homeless. Too many inmates returned to the lives they knew upon release, tougher and savvier than before their incarcerations. He felt law enforcement was brought into the equation too late in the cycle and crime could be prevented by intervening before people considered undertaking a criminal act. In his 2012 interview at USC, Lee said the troubled need someone to believe in them and have "faith in the idea that you're bigger than what your pain is. You have to be something for you before someone can love you for all that you are. . . . My mission is to help people climb out of the things that are getting in the way of their goodness."

The most common crimes plaguing Norwalk were gang violence and vandalism, followed by narcotics. Certain of the power of education and strong role models to change lives and keep kids out of trouble, Lee had continued to fine-tune the Student and the Law classes he had developed as a sergeant. He encouraged his deputies to follow his lead by earning their teaching credentials. Lee worked out an arrangement in which cities paid for the program for their school districts as part of their contracts with the department.

One contract city had a big gang problem. Lee worked with the city to pilot the Deputy Community Specialist Program. The idea was to ease community tensions and humanize the department by having deputies engage out of uniform with local youth. Lee assigned ten of his deputies to tutor and coach high-risk children, teens, and young adults in the Big Brothers Big Sisters–like program. When Lee took command in 1981, the station had fifteen drive-by gang-related shootings. By 1985, the number had dropped to eight. Vandalism had decreased 33 percent and the crime rate, 22. Acknowledging that other youth programs had helped, Lee said, "I can't say it is strictly law enforcement efforts that did this," but added, "You can look around and find a higher degree of public confidence" in the sheriff's department.

Where there is a gang problem, there is a drug problem. The five narcotics investigators at Norwalk were overwhelmed by the sheer volume of cases and tips from residents about heroin and cocaine trafficking. Hours spent testifying in court, interviewing suspects in custody, and processing piles of paperwork kept the detectives from pursuing new leads and working cases. So, Lee brought the managers of the cities he served together and brokered a unique arrangement. Each city agreed to provide additional funding for Norwalk's narcotics unit. Lee was able to double the number of narcotics investigators, hire a secretary for the unit, and procure surveillance vehicles. It was the first

CHAPTER 4

such arrangement in the department and with it, Norwalk's narcotics unit became the largest in the county (most stations' narcotics units had a staff of one to five; Norwalk now had eleven). With the additional resources, the station seized 600 percent more cocaine than the previous year, which came to 25 percent of the entire department's intake.

Almost on par with fighting crime, Lee considered himself in the customer service business. Like any good manager, he wanted to make sure his customers were satisfied. He listened when Norwalk residents complained of harassment, outright neglect in times of need, and a general lack follow-up on the part of the officers. Wanting residents to feel valued, Lee set to reform the station's citizen complaint procedure.

It is known that some law enforcement officers will resort to disreputable practices to protect their brothers in arms from moral and criminal accusations. Interference can be passive-aggressive: general intimidation, not making complaint forms readily available, talking complainants out of filing their grievances, or even tossing completed forms into the nearest trash can. More insidious—especially in an area where many residents are undocumented—is when officers ask for a social security number or search the complainant's history for outstanding warrants before starting the paperwork.

Department policy mandated that all allegations of use of force by deputies be followed up by the captain of their station. But captains were broadly inconsistent as to what they considered excessive and in their recommended discipline. Each captain had their own thermostat for what they deemed inappropriate—for some, it could be a shove; for others, it was anything from a bruise to a broken bone or hospitalization. Captains could dismiss instances they deemed insignificant, thereby keeping a claim from moving up the chain of command for further assessment. Stations operated with an honor system that deputies would voluntarily self-report every use of force, no matter how small, to their captains. Some captains were satisfied with an oral report from their deputies, leaving no lasting record of the incident, while many written reports lacked important details. And when a force incident *was* documented, there was no guarantee it would be included in a deputy's personnel file for consideration of future assignments and promotions. Overall, follow-up with the accused deputy and complainants was negligible, leaving deputies rarely penalized and citizens disenfranchised.

At Norwalk, Lee made it clear that no matter the perceived seriousness of the complaint—from accusations of a disrespectful attitude to those of excessive use of force—his deputies needed to record every incident. If someone Lee had sworn to protect felt maligned in any way, they deserved to be heard. "I don't think we have the highest form of accountability until we account to the individual. They need to have explanations made to them," he said.

It became part of Lee's daily routine to review all the complaints filed at Norwalk. He followed up by personally calling every complainant to see if they were satisfied with the outcome. When a woman was upset that deputies had trampled her roses while chasing a suspect through her garden, Lee bought rose bushes with his own money and went to her house on his day off to plant them. Later in his career, he would say, "Being a captain is the best job in this department . . . because it is the captain who works with people."

It is said that policing is an art, not a science, though it is actually both. As useful as the complaint reports were in following up incidents, they were also a mine of data. As Lee dissected the specifics of each incident, a common theme emerged. He saw most citizen complaints were a product of misunderstanding, animosity, and poor attitudes—from both the public *and* his deputies. In searching for a solution, Lee implemented a progressive approach that was unusual in the LASD or any such paramilitary organization. Complainants were invited to the station to meet with the officer in question, as well as a moderator, to keep the discussion respectful and productive. Removed from the inflammatory situation, these face-to-face meetings gave each participant an opportunity to review what had happened and untangle their words and deeds. Sessions often ended with one side apologizing to the other, and even when they didn't, there was still a sense of resolution. The feedback from his officers, the public, and even the top brass was positive. Lee's progressive system of conflict resolution was further validated when the entire department adopted his procedures, training each watch commander accordingly.

Lee was changing the culture at Norwalk, but out-of-policy use of force was still an issue, as it was throughout law enforcement. Lee had heard too many upsetting stories directly from residents about his own deputies' failures to follow policy. Every large organization has employees who flaunt the rules, but the consequences for poor performance in law enforcement can be grave.

During his time as captain at Norwalk, Lee had collected data on uses of force, intending to use the information to keep it from happening in the future. First he'd identified which deputies had the most complaints against them. (Surprisingly, the department hadn't been documenting this critical statistic.) This alone would inform which deputies needed to be monitored, mentored, retrained, or taken off patrol and training duties.

To understand where and how things were going wrong, he authorized a use-of-force study to identify problems, patterns, and issues regarding department procedures and training. He hoped the information could help create an early warning system of sorts and prevent future breakdowns. Concurrently, he developed a station-level force tracking system. It is all too common in bureaucracies for the right hand not to know what the left is doing. And though reports of force were supposed to be recorded in each station's "black book"—a log of feedback from citizens and supervisors about individual deputies—surprisingly, there was no set policy to ensure each incident was documented nor that the information was added to the deputies' personnel files. In reviewing a deputy's file, it was nearly impossible to know how many times they had been accused of excessive force and how many claims had been substantiated. The information Lee gleaned helped him identify and then personally mentor deputies who were performing below acceptable standards.

On May 24, 1984, the *Los Angeles Times* printed a story about Lee headlined "Sheriff Station Captain More Than Just a Cop." About the innovations introduced at Norwalk Station, Lee explained, "I spend a lot of my time trying to show people who are victimized that we are there to help them. . . . We want to help them restructure their sense of integrity." He told his deputies repeatedly that "when we are being called to the public, they are in a moment of need, and we are their last source of help."

Norwalk council member Peg Nelson concurred when she said, "Lee has made a real effort to communicate with the community. We feel we have immediate response from him. He does not tend to delegate but rather handles things himself." Citizen complaints against Norwalk deputies had dropped from an average of one to two a week to around one a month.

Lee also improved communication *within* the station by setting up a schedule in which subordinates met with their immediate supervisors in a monthly one-on-one parley. Lee met with each of his lieutenants individually, who then met with the station's sergeants, who in turn met with deputies and trainees. Along with the standard pre-shift briefings, this helped ensure everyone's oars were moving in the same direction and provided a regular forum to discuss any concerns, personal or professional.

Though the station had field training officers for deputies new to patrol, Lee also assigned each deputy a primary sergeant for further mentoring, training, and evaluation. The sergeants made sure their newly minted deputies were aware of any unit and departmental changes in policy. Lee also sat down with the deputies in small groups four times a year. With so much of his time now spent as an administrator and chief of police to multiple contract cities, these quarterly four-hour forums kept Lee rooted to what patrol was facing on the streets. Of the one-on-one confabs, Norwalk Lieutenant Joe Monarrez told the *Los Angeles Times*, "We talk about personal problems as well as work problems, and it helps nip them in the bud. . . . It gives people a chance to bring their problems out. And they know they can also talk to us at any time. It's opened the door tremendously. Morale here is very high."

Despite his ever-amassing responsibilities, Lee always made time for education, both his and others. After earning his master's degree, he returned to USC to study for a doctor of public administration. He examined father-daughter incest in his dissertation, having never forgotten a girl from one of his first Student and the Law classes. His intuition had told him something was terribly wrong and he wanted to help. She confided that her father had been abusing her and she was scared and hopeless. Lee confronted the father and later learned he never again touched his daughter.

While earning his PhD, Lee joined the faculty at California State University at Long Beach (CSULB), teaching upper-division police administration and management courses to law enforcement officers and managers and to general students.

The freeways that took Lee the thirty-plus miles from CSULB to his home in Arcadia traversed lands once occupied primarily by the Tongva people. Yaanga, one of their largest villages, was a settlement next to what is now known as the Los Angeles River and is believed to be under US 101. For thousands of years, the land and waters provided the people with deer, small game, fish, and acorns.

All that would change when Spaniard Gaspar de Portolà's 1769 expedition through the West ushered in California's mission era. Furthering the expansion of the Spanish Empire, Franciscan priests traveled north from Mexico and founded twenty-one missions from present-day San Diego to San Francisco in an effort to convert Alta California Native Americans to Christianity. Concurrently, the Spanish military built four presidios to protect the missions' colonizers, churches, and farms. To support the missions and presidios, Las California's governor, Felipe de Neve, authorized the establishment of three civic pueblos.

In 1781, de Neve mobilized a caravan of forty-four intrepid recruits from Sonora and Mazatlán. Half the travelers were children, their parents a mix of Native American, Spanish, Mexican, and African. Recognizing the natural resources the Tongva had at their convenience, they built their settlement right next to them, naming it *El Pueblo de Nuestra Señora la Reina de los Ángeles del Río Porciúncula* (Town of Our Lady the Queen of the Angels of the Porciúncula River).

The pueblo grew rapidly. Soon the surrounding cattle ranches, vineyards, and fields of wheat and vegetables made the area one of the most important agricultural regions in Alta California. Los Angeles was a key provider of beef and food for hundreds of miles, earning the nickname "Queen of the Cow Counties."

In the early 1800s, the first white Americans arrived on whaling ships and overland from the Missouri frontier. The nearby discovery of gold in 1842 in what is now aptly called Placerita Canyon brought a wave of fortune-seekers to the pueblo from all over the US and Europe. Six years later, gold was discovered over three hundred miles to the north, and the California Gold Rush began in earnest. As Los Angeles grew, the Tongva were forcibly evicted and relocated to present-day Boyle Heights.

The burgeoning frontier town earned the dishonor of being the most violent in the West. New Spain had been addressing its crime problem by sending its criminals north. Concurrently, "vigilance committees" in San Francisco and northern mining towns were driving their gamblers, outlaws, and prostitutes south. Fugitives fled to avoid harsh punishments which included branding on the cheek with the letter *R* for

CHAPTER 4

renegade, whippings, and hangings. Marginalized gun-toting ex-soldiers with no one left to fight when the Mexican–American War ended in 1848 joined the desperadoes and fugitives who filled the dusty pueblo's bordellos, saloons, and gambling houses. With such an unsavory mix, it is no wonder the town had a homicide a day. In a 1926 trial, when Wyatt Earp was asked about law and order in Tombstone, Arizona, he replied, "It was not half as bad as Los Angeles."

In 1850, California became the thirty-first state in the Union, necessitating new laws and governing bodies at the state and municipal levels. On April 1 of that year, George T. Burrill was elected for a one-year term as the first sheriff of Los Angeles County. The board of supervisors provided one paid deputy and one jailer, which was a start, but hardly enough manpower to keep the turbulent populace in check. Like other sheriffs in the Wild West, Burrill often joined forces with the city marshal, town constables, and the US Army. A volunteer cavalry militia posse—the Los Angeles Rangers—were also at the ready, and the sheriff had the power to deputize citizens when needed.

When James Barton succeeded Burrill in 1852, outlaws were beginning to realize the power of strength in numbers. Gangs of bandits raped and pillaged the West, stealing horses and cattle, robbing travelers, and murdering at will. When Barton learned the Flores-Daniel Gang was heading towards Los Angeles after a looting, drinking, and killing spree in San Juan Capistrano, he gathered six men and rode south. Near present-day Irvine, the small group was ambushed in a canyon by the fifty-strong gang only to discover someone had removed the ammunition from their guns when they had stopped to rest the previous night. Sheriff Barton and his three deputies were the first Los Angeles lawmen killed in the line of duty.

As the population of Los Angeles increased and urbanization took root, the size and duties of the department changed accordingly as it entered the modern era of policing. By the time Eugene W. Biscailuz took office in 1932, becoming the twenty-seventh sheriff of Los

Angeles County, the term of office had increased from one year to four. Biscailuz served the department for a record fifty-one consecutive years; twenty-six of them as sheriff. Though the public elects the sheriff, Biscailuz had been grooming undersheriff Peter J. Pitchess to take his place. Pitchess was elected in 1959 and, like Biscailuz, stayed in office by winning every election until he was ready to retire. Because it was ultimately up to the voters, there was no guarantee Biscailuz's heir apparent, Lee's friend Sherman Block, would get elected. In a strategic move, Pitchess resigned from office suddenly during his sixth term and convinced the Los Angeles County Board of Supervisors to name Block as his replacement, all but assuring he would be the voters' choice in the next election. It worked. Block was sworn in as sheriff in 1982, when Lee was captain at Norwalk Station.

Chapter 5

Tour De Force

"I will always look at controversy and criticism as an opportunity."

As the custody division was the first stop for newly sworn deputies, it was also a traditional assignment for newly promoted officers. So, when Sheriff Block promoted Lee to commander in 1986, Lee was assigned to Custody Division-Area I, which included the Sybil Brand Institute for Women, the Biscailuz Detention Center, the Hall of Justice Jail (the one-time way station for the likes of Bugsy Siegel, Charles Manson, and Sirhan Sirhan), and the Inmate Services Unit. Like the other county jails, they had been designed to hold misdemeanants serving short sentences, offenders awaiting trial, and convicted prisoners awaiting transport to state prison. Expecting only a third of the population would be violent offenders, the jails were designed as minimum-security facilities with most inmates housed in open, dormitory-like modules or cells of two to four, rather than in individual holding cells.

But the jails' original planners hadn't anticipated the coming upsurge in crime, the explosive growth of violent gangs, and changes in California laws. The wheels of justice moved slowly, increasing jail time and putting more strain on the department's ability to keep up with the influx. Treacherous offenders who needed more supervision and containment had tipped the scales. (Today, they account for almost half the population.) The culture had changed, but the aging infrastructure hadn't. In 1987, a jail system that had been designed for 12,312 inmates housed 22,513. Cells for two slept four and those for four slept eight. Bunks were stacked three high and recreational dayrooms were filled with beds. And when there were no longer enough beds, "floor sleepers" were relegated to mattresses in hallways or chapel pews. Roofs leaked, toilets malfunctioned, and temperature regulation was futile; inmates were uncomfortably hot in the summer and shivering in the winter. There were too many blind spots where prisoners couldn't be seen. Protecting K-10 classified prisoners (High Jail Security Risk) while escorting them through the scores of inmates for court appearances, mealtimes, and visitations required the complete focus of deputies, thereby pulling them from other essential security tasks.

Safe and humane incarceration requires some inmates to be separated from others. Before being assigned to a jail, all inmates are processed through the Inmate Reception Center, which attempts to identify high-risk (violent and dangerous) and vulnerable ("soft") offenders. The reception center also attempts to separate Latino gangs from Black gangs and Crips from Bloods. Public figures, the young and elderly, mentally ill, and homosexuals are housed in separate modules or floors for their own protection. But with six hundred to one thousand bookings a day, it is almost impossible to accommodate each prisoner's needs. Like children playing musical chairs, custody personnel are always scrambling to find an unoccupied spot.

The ideal inmate-to-custodian ratio for jails and prisons is four to one, but during the modern era, in L.A. County jails it can be as high as ten inmates for every guard. Civilians—nonsworn personnel—are employed as custody assistants, but the system still depends on deputies working overtime. Whenever budgets are cut—or when grants and aid from other sources are lost—overtime hours are one of the first expenditures scratched. Next come hiring freezes, which extend deputies' time in custody, demoralizing those who joined the department to fight crime on the streets. When Lee became commander of Sybil Brand, the women's jail, the number of deputies there hadn't increased in at least twelve years, even though the jail was running at double its capacity.

The Los Angeles County jail system is the biggest in the nation. It also holds the dubious title as the country's largest mental institution. Current statistics show 35 percent of the jail system's population is mentally ill. But that's just one comorbid piece in a very grim puzzle. Though the numbers fluctuate year to year, generally half the population has a substance abuse problem and at the time of their arrest were on parole or probation, unemployed, disabled, and/or homeless. A 2008 survey of Sybil Brand found 81 percent had been in jail before, 15 percent of whom had been over ten times. Encumbered by their own circumstances, incarceration is the tragic last stop for these unfortunates. After a series of systemic failures that point to greater societal issues, custody staff is left to pick up the pieces that would be better handled by mental health professionals.

The average stay for inmates in the L.A. County jails fluctuates from year to year. In 1983, it was 23.6 days. By 1995, it climbed to 35, with third-strikers staying as long as 226. As a newly minted custody commander, Lee saw an opportunity to solve three endemic problems in the jails: outbreaks of violence due to overcrowding and boredom, difficulties inmates face reentering society upon release, and recidivism. For someone who lived every second of his day to the fullest, it broke Lee's heart seeing prisoners disengaged and wasting the hours away watching television or in mundane or negative conversation. It was clear these souls needed someone to believe in them. Lee did, and because of the personal successes he had witnessed in the classroom as a student and a teacher, he believed education was a critical component in rendering a solution.

To determine what kind of program would be most effective in addition to the vocational training already offered, Lee organized a literacy survey of the jail population. The data revealed a sorry 38 percent illiteracy level; for comparison, the national average is 1 percent. So, Lee established a team of educators, deputies, and volunteers to develop a computer-aided literacy program. Starting any new program was challenging in an institution always strapped for cash. To launch the program, it was up to Lee to figure out how to pay for it. The Inmate Welfare Fund generated revenue from prisoner commissary sales, payphones, and hobby craft sales. These profits were used for food, building maintenance, training, clothing, and other supplies and services. After crunching the numbers, Lee figured out how to direct some vocational training funds to the new literacy program without sacrificing the former. Expanding educational programming in the jails became a cornerstone of Lee's tradition of service.

Lee was reassigned to command Field Operations Region III in 1988. During his years there, the department faced some of the biggest challenges and scandals in its history of service. In February 1990, ten sheriff deputies were indicted by a grand jury on charges of stealing more than $1.4 million during narcotics raids. Three months later, the *Los Angeles Times* published a front-page exposé citing incidents where blatant and senseless excessive force by deputies against people of color cost the county $8.5 million in major settlements and jury awards in a three-year period. The piece listed numerous cases when routine calls and stops escalated into inexplicable uses of force and ended with significant civilian injuries and, in the worst cases, death. Sheriff Block came off as uncooperative and dismissive but, notably, the following

CHAPTER 5

month he assembled a task force to study the department's application of force. A series of scandals and controversial shootings would later prompt other agencies to conduct thorough examinations of the LASD.

In September 1990, the NAACP and Educational Defense Fund filed a civil rights class-action lawsuit against the department, alleging that deputies of South Central's Lynwood Station "systematically engaged in racial abuse, beatings, unjustified shootings, and other unlawful conduct," and that Lynwood Station was home to a covert "neo-Nazi, white supremacist gang" of LASD deputies who routinely and purposefully violated citizens' freedoms.

For centuries, firsthand accounts of racial profiling and police abuse were endemic in minority communities, but their cries for accountability and justice were rarely heard or heeded. That was until a nine-minute-and-twenty-second video shot by a plumbing salesman played in a loop on living room TVs across the globe.

On the evening of March 3, 1991, George Holliday was awakened around one a.m. by screeching tires, police sirens, and a low-flying helicopter circling above his apartment in the northeastern San Fernando Valley. Having recently purchased a new camcorder, he grabbed it as he stepped onto his balcony to see what was going on. Holliday was about to shoot the most watched and analyzed footage since the Zapruder film of the Kennedy assassination.

A high-speed chase had come to an end with four LAPD officers brutally beating a Black motorist named Rodney King while ten others stood by and watched. Police tased, kicked, and struck King with their batons over fifty times. When four of the charged LAPD officers were acquitted for use of excessive force just over a year after the incident, the City of Angels erupted. The verdict's announcement was followed by six days of looting, arson, and mayhem, including a brutal and random revenge attack on a white truck driver. The LAPD were ill-equipped to handle the unrest and sheer number of crimes. The National Guard was called in to help restore order. The riots concluded with sixty-three dead, 2,383 injured, and twelve thousand arrested. Property damage was estimated to be over $1 billion. But the damage to the city and nation's psyche was unquantifiable.

In the summer of 1991, four controversial killings in a four-week period sent relations between the LASD and the public to a new nadir. All the victims were Latino or Black. At Ramona Gardens, an East Los Angeles housing project under LAPD jurisdiction, nineteen-year-old Arturo Jimenez was killed by an out-of-jurisdiction LASD deputy, inciting a violent five-hour standoff between officers and residents. Ten days later, Keith Hamilton, a man with a mental illness, was shot in the back eight times and killed by two sheriff's deputies. And when a deputy thought fifteen-year-old David Angel Ortiz was reaching for a gun, he killed the suspected auto thief in a "waistband shooting," less than a week after the Hamilton shooting. On Labor Day, Steve Clemons was shot in the back while running from sheriff's deputies in a park after they reported to complaints of a gang disturbance.

Three days after Clemons was killed, the FBI launched an investigation into the department's policies regarding use of force and civil rights violations. Shortly thereafter, District Attorney Ira Reiner announced the Los Angeles County Grand Jury would investigate all four shootings.

Just as Mayor Tom Bradley had formed the Christopher Commission to fully examine the LAPD in the wake of the Rodney King beating, the Board of Supervisors of Los Angeles County appointed special counsel—retired Superior Court Judge James G. Kolts—to head a commission examining "the policies, practices and procedures of the sheriff's department, including recruitment, training, job performance and evaluation, record keeping and management practices, as they relate to allegations of excessive force, the community sensitivity of deputies and the department's citizen complaint procedure."

Kolts and a staff of over sixty attorneys, CPAs, sociologists, and

CHAPTER 5

other professionals left no stone unturned in their six-month inquiry. The commission reviewed hundreds of thousands of records and probed 124 cases of excessive force. Over three public hearings, they interviewed witnesses to force incidents and listened to the concerns of citizens and community groups. Additionally, over a hundred current and past LASD employees testified before the committee, including Commander Lee Baca.

Released in July 1992, the 359-page report's principal finding was that "within the LASD there is deeply disturbing evidence of excessive force and lax discipline." Yet Kolts and his team didn't find evidence to support the public perception that most officers were racist and violent, writing:

> Our investigation leads us to believe that nearly all deputies treat nearly all individuals, most of the time, with at least minimally acceptable levels of courtesy and dignity. The exceptions, when they occur, are outrageous enough and frequent enough to poison the well in some communities. The perception becomes the reality. The LASD must understand that one racial slur or incident of unreasonable force reverberates quickly throughout a community and can undermine years of work to build up trust between the LASD and its constituency.

Rather than being driven by malice or personal anger, they surmised, most deputies' misconduct was the result of their creating no-win situations through negligence, poor training, and bad decision-making prompted by misperceiving the levels of threat in any given situation.

But by no means did Kolts and his team give the department a clean bill of health.

"This report is a somber and sobering one in terms of the large number of brutal incidents that have been and still are occurring," they wrote. One of their most disturbing discoveries was that in a department of eight thousand sworn personnel, sixty-two deputies were responsible for almost five hundred separate use-of-force and harassment incidents. Yet, because the department had no system in place to monitor deputies' performance over time, no one knew. Not only did repeat offenders stay on duty, but they were assigned as training officers to new and impressionable academy graduates and promoted ill-deservedly.

The report also took issue with how the department handled citizens' complaints of excessive force. They determined the process of filing a complaint was unnecessarily difficult, often intimidating, and sometimes the complainants were hassled and threatened. Responses to complaints varied from station to station. Stations' investigations were slow, with almost no follow-up with the complainants as to what disciplinary actions had been taken. With no civilian oversight (per the California Constitution), the LASD was left to monitor itself. Many people, especially those in Black and Latino communities, found the department unresponsive and had lost confidence in its ability to police itself.

The Kolts Report concluded with a list of recommendations for the department, including:

1. Making it perfectly clear throughout the chain of command that excessive force will not be tolerated whatsoever.

2. Developing an early warning system by documenting and tracking every claim of excessive force, no matter how big or small, to identify, discipline, retrain, and/or remove problem deputies.

3. Implementing a more welcoming and thorough system for citizen complaints, starting at the station level.

4. Rapidly expanding community policing at each station.

5. Ensuring employees are tolerant of race, gender, ethnicity, and sexual orientation both within the workplace and with the public.

The Los Angeles County Board of Supervisors found the Kolts Report so valuable that it engaged Kolts's special counsel, Merrick Bobb, to continue examining the department. Bobb and his team would issue thirty-four semiannual reports between October 1993 and August 2014. Over the years, they unveiled major inconsistencies and shortcomings in how the department documented force incidents.

Lee had spent hours working with the Kolts Commission, and when he read the report, he was disappointed but not surprised by the harsh review of his beloved department. At the same time, he was heartened by their recommendations, many of which affirmed the work he had already undertaken to improve the relationship between the department and citizens, as well as his efforts to reduce the number of force incidents. In fact, Lee was one of the few officers singled out by Kolts and recognized for his innovations regarding citizens' complaints and tracking use of force. While other police departments scrambled to address issues of excessive force in response to the Rodney King incident, Lee had already been working on the question for a decade.

When he became commander of Region III, Lee continued building on what he had started at Norwalk, leading teams to address the overall question of use of force department-wide. He oversaw the establishment of a Force Review Planning Committee, which examined all investigations into exceptional use of force and recommended the appropriate response to improve deputies' future performances. And as vice chairman of the Department Training Committee, Lee directed the Force Training Unit, which revised policy and established certification based on a scale of escalation and a reverence for life threshold.

Lee was essential in building an early warning system to anticipate and prevent uses of force by asking questions such as: Did the department's policies regarding use of force need to be clarified or better communicated? Did some partners bring out the worst in each other? Did time of day play a factor? Who was the faulted deputy's training officer? Which weapons were used—flashlights, batons, saps, or fists—and on which body parts? Were the disciplinary measures and consequences for violations of the department's use of force policy effective and uniformly enforced?

Analyzing use of force and implementing new policies was a massive undertaking, requiring manpower and funding. At the station level, the time spent documenting force incidents and writing extra reports would keep supervisors from other responsibilities. And while deputies were taken off their shifts for compulsory training, others would need to fill their spots, necessitating overtime pay or new hires.

The decades-long problem wasn't unique to the LASD and the proposed solutions would be slow to take hold. A Venn diagram of how many divisions and bureaus within the department and how many outside agencies were needed to bring about any change in the bureaucracy would look like a mandala drawn by a three-year-old—or perhaps hundreds of three-year-olds, each oblivious to what the others were doing. Hundreds of academy instructors, numerous specialized units, and the unique needs of sundry divisions and bureaus made uniform departmental change all the more difficult. The department's *Manual of Policy and Procedures* (currently at seven volumes and over 1,700 pages long) would need to be updated and all changes made known through the ranks, from the sheriff himself to new academy trainees.

CHAPTER 5

And the buck didn't necessarily stop with the sheriff. In theory, the sheriff of Los Angeles County can run and reform the department as he sees fit, but in reality, a number of outside agencies have a voice. The Board of Supervisors holds the purse strings and determines the department's annual budget. The district attorney decides when to press criminal charges against a member of the department and which cases to pursue. The Civil Service Commission hears and can overturn departmental-determined discipline meted out to personnel. The Association for Los Angeles Deputy Sheriffs and the Los Angeles County Professional Peace Officers Association Union advocate for their members and work to protect their civil and workplace rights. The department must adhere to California Peace Officer Standards and Training mandates, and the jails to the Department of Justice.

As commander of Field Operations Region III, Lee supervised the captains of six stations on the eastern side of Los Angeles County as well as Avalon Station on Santa Catalina Island. Region III also served a number of contract cities and unincorporated communities, encompassing a jurisdiction of 543 square miles and almost a million citizens. Lee managed a $111 million budget—almost twice that of his last assignment—and 1,500 personnel. On top of that, he oversaw the Aero and Special Enforcement bureaus and executed over fifty Special Weapons Team deployments dealing with armed, barricaded suspects. He commanded pursuits, investigations, officer-involved shootings, complaints, performance reviews, jail standards, and use of force activity. Lee also became active on the department's diversity committee and somehow, still found time to work on his doctorate.

Though department insiders thought Sheriff Block was grooming Lee to take the helm when he retired, Lee wasn't so sure. Friends, coworkers, and community leaders encouraged him to run against Block in the next election, but he struggled with the idea. He respected and appreciated Block's mentorship over the years, yet he was frustrated that Block seemed to address problems *after* a mishandled incident or scandal, rather than taking proactive measures to keep them from happening in the first place. Lee also recognized how much farther the department needed to go to fully embrace community-based policing. And while Block had made efforts to steer the department in that direction, at his core he and his inner circle were old-school, instilled in professional policing ways and slow to accept unconventional ideas. And Lee Baca had always had plenty of unconventional ideas.

An advocate of outreach programming, Lee enlisted the help of the Black Peace Officer Association and team-developed Self-Education Law Enforcement Family (SELF) classes for Black male youths. Volunteer Black deputy sheriffs taught a ten-week curriculum built around the seven principles of Kwanzaa: self-determination, collective work and responsibility, cooperative economics, purpose, creativity, unity, and faith. Lee cultivated a partnership with the Southern Area Clergy Council to bring the program to area churches, including a Church of Christ in Willowbrook, a neighborhood between Watts and Compton.

Driven by the success of SELF, Lee worked with community leaders from the gang-ridden area to develop more programming for at-risk youth. He developed the Sheriff's Youth Athletic League (YAL) at the Willowbrook church, which soon expanded to youth centers and local parks. YAL activities grew to include tutoring, drama, dance, computer classes, and one-on-one mentorships.

Lee also built a partnership with the Los Angeles chapter of Men Against Destruction Defending Against Drugs and Social Disorder (MAD DADS). Founded in 1989 by a group of Nebraskan fathers fed up with rampant gang violence and illegal drugs in their community, the organization placed volunteers on foot patrol to deter crime and serve as positive role models. A 1995 *Los Angeles Times* article put it this way: "Taking the concept of 'community policing' to its fullest, the group hits the streets to contact runaways, drug abusers, gang members and troubled youths." The LASD developed a thirteen-week community-policing training program for MAD DADS volunteers.

Lee encouraged his subordinates at different stations to be innovative in creating programs for their communities. Because every penny in the department's budget was already allocated, if Lee wanted to expand an existing program or launch a new one, it was up to him to chase down the funding. He hit up corporations, nonprofits, and local businesses for donations or grants, and also sought state assistance. When he spoke to community groups, he pled a convincing case. In one three-year period, Lee sought and received $1.1 million of discretionary funds from County Supervisor Yvonne Brathwaite Burke for community-based policing programs. This provided two mobile command posts for deployment in high-crime areas, as well as bicycles, volunteer patrol vehicles, and a state-of-the-art computer network designed to manage problems in certain neighborhoods.

Community problems weren't confined to the inner city, nor was Lee's attention. Following a spate of verbal and physical assaults by Latino youth against Orthodox Jews in the San Fernando Valley, community leaders reached out to the LAPD for help, but got little response. Seeking to improve relations between Jews and Latinos, the B'nai B'rith Anti-Defamation League formed the Latino-Jewish Roundtable. When Lee heard, he organized and co-chaired a Latino-Jewish Unity Day luncheon, raising nearly $15,000 for multicultural school programs. He subsequently became so involved with EMEK Hebrew Academy (which was in an area patrolled by the LAPD) that the school invited him to be an honorary member of its board. Rabbi Eliezer Eidlitz said of Lee's support for the construction of a $3.3 million facility, "He's a one-man cheering squad. We had been talking about a new building for eight years, but his words crystallized our determination to move ahead."

When rumors began that the Los Angeles Board of Police

Commissioners was looking to replace LAPD Chief Daryl Gates after the Rodney King debacle, Lee's friends and supporters urged him to leave the sheriff's department and apply for Gates's position. The Latino community in particular wanted Lee for the job. In the LAPD's 116-year history, the chief had always been white. Lee knew he could make a difference in the LAPD. And he knew he was ready for the top position. The opportunity to restore the LAPD from its lowest moment in history and guide it toward community policing was appealing.

The irony of becoming chief after failing the entrance exam when he was eighteen wasn't lost on Lee. Three days after the Christopher Commission released its report on the Rodney King incident and called for his removal, Gates announced his retirement in July 1991.

Lee decided he wanted the job. So did thirty others. A seven-member panel of community leaders narrowed the field to a dozen candidates. Lee made the cut. The panel then rated each candidate with composite scores based on interviews and testing. Lee received ninety-four points out of a hundred. With the third-highest score, boosted by his experience and vast knowledge of the city, Lee felt confident he'd get the position. His ambitions were unexpectedly brought to a halt, however, by an antiquated city charter provision that favored LAPD "insiders." Under this scoring system, Lee dropped from third to seventh place and was eliminated.

The Latino community and its leaders were outraged. Lee told the *Los Angeles Times* the rule was "deeply divisive" and "bureaucratic protectionism." He appealed the decision, but was denied. Angry, Lee licked his wounds and moved on. His time would come.

In 1992, the LASD had eight different divisions, each headed by a chief. When Lee was promoted to chief of the LASD's Court Services Division, he was the highest-ranking Latino in the department. Above

CHAPTER 5

him were the sheriff himself, the undersheriff, and two assistant sheriffs. The Court Services Division provides security and support services for the Los Angeles County Superior Court, the largest general jurisdiction in the country. At the time, the county had twenty Superior Court Facilities and jails and 238 judges.

The Court Services Division is also responsible for one of the largest prisoner transportation systems in the nation. In 1992, approximately two thousand prisoners were shuttled back and forth every day between jail and court and state prisons. The LASD also contracted with the LAPD and thirty-two counties to provide prisoner transportation. Accounting for the security of staff and prisoners was a Herculean task, both administratively and physically.

As he had done with every new position, Lee wrote a vision statement for his role: "To provide the Superior Court System with a high level of quality service that respects the authority of each court, prosecutor, defense attorney, clerk, and participant by ensuring each deputy sheriff is trained, supervised, and empowered to be a member of a service team directed by Superior Court Judges."

To accomplish this, Lee conceptualized and directed the development of Quality Service Plans for each court. His department surveyed judges, clerks, prosecutors, defense attorneys, and court administrators to assess their individual needs. Deputies then customized a plan of action for each court. As he had on patrol—and in every aspect of his life—Lee considered it his duty to find out what service was needed, then do his best to provide it.

Since 1952, the Los Angeles County Marshal's Department had been responsible for courtroom security, custody control, and the service of bench warrants issued by *municipal* courts in Los Angeles County, while the sheriff's department did the same work for the *superior* courts. There had long been talk that the overlap between the two agencies was fiscally unsound. A 1994 study ordered by the Board of

Supervisors confirmed that folding the nine hundred personnel of the Los Angeles County Marshal into the LASD would save the county money.

As the new chief of Court Services, Lee led the management team that developed budgetary, legislative, and staffing strategies to engineer the merger. Marshal's department employees were found new positions in the LASD, and when all was said and done, the county saved $15 million a year in duplicate administrative costs. For his efforts, Lee was honored with the department's Distinguished Service Award.

With a pending transfer to chief of Field Operations Region II in 1994, Lee trained former Marshal Robert Mann to assume his position as chief of Court Services. During Lee's tenure, the division's budget had grown from $70 million to $114 million and the staff had increased to 1,400 employees, serving twice as many courts.

Chapter 6

Community Building

"I'm not 'sort of' a social worker; I am a social worker."

After thirty years of marriage, Lee and Judith divorced in 1994. Lee moved into a condo in downtown Pasadena and also a new office in Dominguez Hills upon his appointment to chief of Field Operations Region II.

His new command encompassed approximately eighty-two square miles, including the areas served by the West Hollywood, Lennox-Marina del Rey, Century, Carson, and Lomita stations; eight contract cities; and thirteen unincorporated communities. Lee led 1,300 personnel. The scope of his job was comparable to running a major police department. To put things in perspective, Cincinnati, Ohio, is less than eighty square miles and, in 2010, its police department had approximately 1,200 employees.

Reporting directly to the assistant sheriff, Lee annually inspected each station to ensure they were operating up to standards. He checked jails, vehicle fleets, computer systems, emergency operations and plans, records, and more for weaknesses and strengths. During these inspections, he asked question after question of volunteers, civilian employees, trainees, and supervisors wanting to hear about their experiences, complaints, and ideas for improvement and how he could help.

Upon attaining his new role, one of Lee's first acts was to send a memo to his commanders and captains with the subject "Service Oriented Management—Ethics in Leadership." Adhering to his own principle that "listening is the ultimate quality of leadership," Lee outlined tactics for resolving conflict and improving communication. The idea was rooted in the premise that if deputies felt supported and cared for by their superiors and learned conflict resolution through firsthand experiences, they would carry the skills with them on the streets and be better public servants. In his memo, Lee encouraged managers to "make a continuous and consistently positive impact on all staff and supervisory personnel through the chain of command." He maintained that heightened states of conflict would deescalate when subordinates felt heard by their superiors. The memo included a list of points that offers insight into Lee's holistic views and might strike some as unusual advice coming from a law enforcement leader:

- Seek to empower others with your presence, guidance, and understanding.
- Avoid losing your integrity by denying another his or her integrity.
- Handle your own stress in a manner that does not increase your subordinate's stress.
- Seek to balance your life so your self-esteem is relatively secure.
- Take sincere joy in the success of your subordinates, peers, and superiors.
- Retain a vigorous pursuit of art, music, philosophy, politics, anthropology, and culture.

CHAPTER 6

- Respect, admire, and feel in awe of the outstanding examples of leadership, self-management, problem-solving, and human kindness exhibited by line-level personnel.

Lee also directed each of his stations to produce a Quality Service Plan to create a positive working environment. Topics included principles and procedures for leadership, conflict resolution, personnel development, accountability, and reward and recognition. Lee's theory of problem-solving was to "delegate the leadership role down to the bottom," so each deputy was briefed by a sergeant on the plan and given a personal copy of it. It was imperative that everyone was on the same page.

In his new position, Lee had the autonomy to reform the culture and operations of his division by introducing new community policing ideas. His vision was to "integrate community resources with the sheriff's department to improve the quality of life for individuals, races, ethnic groups, neighborhoods, businesses, and communities."

Each station in his region served a very different clientele. A one-size-fits-all approach wouldn't accommodate each community's different needs. As he had done as captain at Norwalk, he asked his captains to outline their communities' main policing concerns and how they planned to fix them. Lee's efforts were commended in the second semiannual study special counsel Merrick Bobb released pursuant to the Kolts Report:

> With the notable exception of Region II, where Chief Lee Baca and Commanders Ashby and King have required each station to prepare a Quality Service Plan, these important recommendations [from the Kolts Report] do not appear to have been implemented. Because Region II has begun to think about these issues, and service plans have actually been produced . . . we

recommend that the experiment taking place in Region II be emulated throughout the department.

The city of West Hollywood in particular demanded a customized program. Home to the Sunset Strip, Santa Monica and Beverly Boulevards, and Robertson and Melrose Avenues, West Hollywood has been called the most walkable city in California. In a county known for its lack of pedestrians, West Hollywood is an exception, which necessitates a patrol plan unlike any other community. Until 1984, when it became its own city, West Hollywood was an unincorporated area served by the sheriff's department. In the days of Prohibition, gambling was outlawed in the city of Los Angeles, but legal in the county. And though the sale of alcohol was forbidden in both, the LASD was less inclined to enforce dry laws than the more vigilant LAPD. Speakeasies and casinos sprouted up along the Sunset Strip. Partly because of its proximity to the wealthy in Beverly Hills and Bel Air, the area appealed to interior design firms and fashion houses. Personal expression and freedom came to define West Hollywood.

In 1991, 10 percent of West Hollywood's population was Russian immigrants, 20 percent was senior citizens, and 20 percent was gay or lesbian. Homosexuality was a crime in California until 1964. And with a permissiveness similar to its indifference to illegal liquor, the LASD was markedly less zealous in enforcing the law than the LAPD. The latter was known to frequently raid gay bars, and in 1963 alone, arrested over three thousand men for homosexual behavior. Under the LASD's eyes, gays and lesbians felt safer in West Hollywood, and if they didn't live there, came for the nightlife and social scene.

Before Lee became chief of Region II, West Hollywood had been debating severing its relationship with the LASD in favor of forming its own police department. It was a contract the department couldn't afford to lose. West Hollywood paid the LASD $8.4 million a year for its services—a tenth of the department's contract city income.

CHAPTER 6

But anecdotal evidence of offensive and demeaning behavior from deputies directed toward gay men had been substantiated when the Kolts Report affirmed the department indeed had an anti-gay bias. By 1994, efforts were in place to improve the department's standing in the gay community, within the department itself, and on the streets. In a belated attempt at diplomacy, Sheriff Block attended a gay pride parade, but the crowd jeered at him.

As the new chief of Region II, Lee made West Hollywood one of his top priorities. He worked closely with city and community leaders to hear their concerns and what they wanted from the sheriff's department. One complaint was that deputies circulated in and out of the station too frequently to establish any meaningful relationship with the citizens. Lee reduced turnover at the station and sent the newly consistent deputies door-to-door to introduce themselves to residents and hand out business cards so they could be reached directly. Lee also initiated a successful campaign to recruit gays and lesbians to the department. In a 1998 interview with *L.A. Weekly*, a West Hollywood councilman credited Lee for turning the city "into a model of community-based policing" and that Lee "made the department attuned to the need of the community. It set an example for community outreach that's been followed since, elsewhere in the county."

Law enforcement is generally not the culture that comes to mind when one thinks of workplace sensitivity to homosexuality. Lee had been an instructor in the department's diversity training program, which had always focused on racism and sexism. When Lee added homophobia to the curriculum, his advocacy engendered derision and backhanded remarks. Unruffled, he began mentoring gay and lesbian deputies throughout the department, not just in Region II. He asked one of the only two openly gay deputies in the department to conduct cultural awareness training, which included lessons on stereotypes, hate crimes, offensive terminology, and workplace collaboration. Of the success in West Hollywood, councilman John Duran said, "As a former civil rights lawyer who sued the sheriff's department every chance he got, I've seen a drastic change. They have done exactly what they said they would: They reformed."

Merrick Bobb's second semiannual report on the department corroborated:

> The West Hollywood Station . . . proposes a community satisfaction survey, among other good ideas, and requires that the [sic] all sworn personnel at the station actively attend community meetings and events to provide an effective liaison and sounding board for community access to the sheriff's department. The plan lists a broad variety of community organizations that will be included, from the City Council and Chamber of Commerce to two different gay and lesbian organizations, a Senior Citizen's council, and the Chabad Russian program.

Lee was also sensitive to the difficulties female deputies faced. Women were disproportionately underrepresented in the male-dominant field, and overt sexual harassment and discrimination were chronic. The Kolts Report stated, "Like minorities, women deputies appear to suffer from a double standard. If a woman deputy is ambitious, she is labeled as having 'an attitude.' There is a widespread feeling that 'women have to be twice as good' to prove themselves and that any mistake made by a woman receives much more attention than if the mistake were made by a man." The department had been trying to recruit more women, but as few had risen to positions of authority, advancement seemed impossible.

Raised by a formidable woman, Lee knew women were well able to handle the demands of the job and lead just as well—or, in his words, "twice as good"—than many of the men he had seen promoted over the years. He had always been especially impressed by Helena Ashby, who shared his work ethic, conviction in community policing, and reverence for education. The African American woman was a fellow USC alum who had earned a master's degree from Harvard's Kennedy School of Government. She had graduated from the sheriff's academy a year before Lee—back when women were issued white shirts, knee-length skirts, two-inch pumps, and shoulder purses to carry their guns and handcuffs. She'd celebrated when the first women graduated from patrol school in 1972; until then, women had been relegated to desk jobs, women's jail, and juvenile investigations.

Ashby had worked her way up through the ranks from being the first woman deputy assigned to the Sheriff's Community Relations Bureau, where she engaged with Black militant groups to manage protests and avoid riots in the late 1960s, to becoming captain of the Juvenile Investigations Bureau, Court Services West, Sybil Brand Institute for Women, and the Personnel Bureau. She had risen to the rank of commander of the Detective Division and Field Operations Region II, the highest position a woman had ever held in the department. But five years in, Ashby had hit the department's glass ceiling.

Lee held Ashby in high regard. She was a strong, principled, and compassionate leader, and one of the organization's brightest stars. Not only had Ashby been lauded by the special counsel team for the Quality Service Plans she had overseen in Region II, but in their December 1994 report, she was distinguished as the only commander who had followed up with the Data Systems Bureau on the information collected on citizens' complaints and use of force—one of the most critical issues the LASD had been advised to reform.

Critics had long complained that promotions in the department were not given to the most qualified candidates but to those who worked the "good ol' boy" network. Becoming a sergeant or lieutenant was a straightforward process based on a civil service test. Those with the highest scores were promoted first. Yet openings for higher positions weren't always posted but rather shared by word of mouth and given to those with high-level influential connections in the department. Too often they came from political savvy, not necessarily merit. One had to know how to play the game. Lee believed in Ashby, even when she didn't believe in herself. As her mentor, he emboldened her to "make herself known" (in department lingo) to those who mattered. On her own merit—and with Lee's tutelage—Ashby became the first female chief in the LASD.

Lee had been collecting and analyzing the data on deputies' use of force as a captain and commander when he served on the Force Review Committee and Force Training Unit. Stymied by decades of poor record keeping, he had developed a Use of Force Tracking System to build a comprehensive picture of all the factors at play. When the Kolts Commission had reviewed the LASD's chaotic and failing records management, they found it was actually intentional, reporting: "Driven by fears that data on use of force and citizen complaints would be used against it in civil litigation, the LASD followed legal advice from County Counsel to avoid creating 'paper trails' when it could. When it could not, the information was scattered throughout the LASD and kept haphazardly."

In special counsel Bobb's semiannual report published seven years later, Lee was recognized as "a vigorous and convincing advocate for accountability both within the LASD and in numerous conversations with Judge Kolts and his staff." Lee helped develop a groundbreaking system—the Personnel Performance Index (PPI)—to:

1. Record deputies' uses of force, disciplinary history, litigation outcomes, and commendations and complaints against them from within the department and from citizens.

CHAPTER 6

2. Monitor and compare individual patrol stations.

3. Centralize data from claims, lawsuits, and internal investigations.

Creating the PPI was a monumental undertaking. A database, software, and server needed to be created and maintained. Patrol stations needed computer upgrades, and personnel (already overextended from hiring freezes and budget cuts) needed data entry training. The initiative received tremendous resistance at the station level. Supervisors balked at the extra paperwork and deputies worried the data would be misused. For example, every complaint voiced by a citizen would be documented and tallied, no matter how frivolous; lawsuits filed by multiple citizens on a single incident could appear as multiple separate incidents; if a deputy was acquitted of misconduct, would it be noted in the database?; was it fair to deputies working "fast" stations in more violent neighborhoods who would likely have more force incidents than those at quieter stations?

Bobb's report stated, "The PPI, without question, is the most carefully constructed and powerful management tool for control of police misconduct currently available in the United States." Law enforcement agencies across the country recognized the innovative system as a powerful tool for inquiry, investigation, and intervention, and reached out to the LASD to purchase or license the program.

But the PPI would only be valuable if the information gathered was used effectively. As in any large bureaucracy, the left hand often didn't know what the right was doing, and sometimes the only answer was to add yet another department. Lee helped create the Risk Management Bureau, which created channels of communication between Internal Affairs and Internal Criminal Investigations to review claims against the department. The database was fluid, adding or amending categories as need arose. To broaden the platform he was building, Lee developed an Investigative Case Management program for the detectives at each station to record cases, court filings, district attorney rejections, and arrest data.

As chief of Region II, Lee made it his policy to personally interview each deputy under his command who had made the critical decision to fire his weapon in the line of duty. Each situation was far more than the data gathered and reports generated. Through first-hand accounts Lee was better able to understand, assess, and support his men and women.

All the while, Lee used his position to steer the department to a model of community policing. Expanding on the Quality Service Plans he had developed as a captain and introduced to the courts and Region II stations, he developed a department-wide Community-Based Policing Program for contract cities and unincorporated areas.

As Lee sought to expand programming, bean counters at the Board of Supervisors were scrambling to keep the county afloat. In trying to resolve its own budget imbalance, the state cut approximately $1 billion from the county over a two-year period. Coupled with slow growth in local taxes and pay increases, the county faced a $1.16 billion deficit in 1993. Sheriff Block warned that the $152-million proposed cut to his department would result in jail closures, layoffs, and the release of thousands of prisoners.

Undeterred by the bleak picture, Lee understood that if he wanted to introduce new programs it would be up to him to secure the financing. He began applying for every federal, state, and private grant he could find. He won thirteen, bringing in $10 million. Lee was making friends in high places and building a network of influence from Sacramento to Washington, DC that would provide personal and professional support over the years ahead. He had signed up to be a cop, but along the journey had become a social worker, and it seemed, a politician too.

Chapter 7

Taking the Plunge

"The public owns this department. We are just the caretakers."

Influential Latinos had been watching Lee's ascent through the ranks and were hopeful the Mexican American from East L.A. would head either the city's or county's law enforcement agency one day. A longtime resident of the San Gabriel Valley, Lee found further encouragement from the area's growing Asian community. He had been a regular and visible presence at cultural festivals and events and in civic and professional associations, through which he had developed enduring personal relationships.

It was at the Chinese Club of San Marino's annual Autumn Club Festival in November 1996 that Lee met Carol Chiang. Upon first setting eyes on the Taiwanese-born beauty, Lee was smitten. Carol was the most striking women in the room. One attendee compared her to a model. After asking Carol to dance, Lee was further charmed by her intelligence, gentle nature, and wit. To boot, she had a master's degree

SHERIFF LEE BACA

in computer engineering from his alma mater, USC. During that first dance, Carol was captivated by the tall, dark, handsome gentleman who radiated goodness and grace. She was taken with Lee's candidness as he told her about his divorce and alimony payments. They soon fell in love. In a show of his devotion to her, Lee began learning Chinese. Carol became Lee's staunchest advocate.

Lee wanted to be sheriff. He'd made that clear to Sherman Block, hoping his longtime mentor would "anoint" him as his heir apparent, as the last two sheriffs, Biscailuz and Pitchess, had done for their successors. When Lee had been appointed to Region II in 1994, the sixty-nine-year-old war horse was just beginning his fourth four-year term. Block had successfully appealed to the Board of Supervisors to revoke a resolution mandating elected officials retire at seventy. Though the Latino and Asian communities had been encouraging Lee to run for sheriff in 1998, he didn't want to square off against his mentor. He had too much respect for Block, and knew challenging him would create discord and tension in an institution that valued loyalty.

Once again, leadership of the LAPD was at another turning point. After a series of scandals, it seemed the city would be looking for another new chief. It was no secret that Mayor Richard Riordan, Tom Bradley's successor, was dissatisfied with Chief Willie Williams and unlikely to renew his contract for another five-year term. In 1997, the police commission began looking for someone who could turn the department around. The rule that had given LAPD insiders a leg up in the testing phase and led to Lee's disqualification in 1992 had since been revoked. Though the idea of leaving the sheriff's department after thirty-two years kindled an internal conflict in Lee, he knew he had to try again, recognizing the new position as "a chance for a great partnership between the sheriff's department and the LAPD." As he had five years earlier, he made it to the list of six semifinalists.

In truth, a part of Lee was relieved when he learned the position was to be awarded to Bernard Parks. As much as Lee had wanted the job,

CHAPTER 7

leaving the sheriff's department would have been bittersweet. Sherman Block was aging and in poor health. Lee could run for sheriff when he retired, which had to be soon.

Sure enough, as Block's fourth term was coming to a close, he told his confidants he wouldn't seek a fifth. Lee and a few other department members decided to run for his seat. But Block waffled. In October 1997, at seventy-three years old, waving a list of endorsements, the ailing sheriff declared his candidacy for reelection. Block had survived both non-Hodgkin's lymphoma and prostate cancer, had high blood pressure, and underwent dialysis treatment three times a week for kidney damage sustained from chemotherapy. Many worried he wouldn't survive a fifth term. While the other insiders immediately dropped out of the race, Lee held firm, concerned about who the supervisors would appoint sheriff should Block perish while in office.

Block was confident no one could beat him. The last time an incumbent sheriff had lost reelection in Los Angeles County was 1914. Despite the scandals of recent years, he was well-liked by voters and was part of the county's status quo. The other contenders had little name recognition and didn't have his access to big donors. Nevertheless, it would be the first time Block faced any significant opposition.

Lee, Block, and two other hopefuls faced off for the first time in a March 1998 debate that was closed to the press and the public. Hosted by the deputies' union ALADS, around 130 attended the ninety-minute event, in which Lee said, "Sheriff Block, you have done many good things for this department . . . I know you love the department and want it to prosper. But it is time for a change. Respectfully, I ask you to reconsider your decision [to run]. Allow this department to move forward."

Ever since the department's narcotics scandal at the beginning of the decade, Block had been playing Whac-A-Mole, battering one public relations crisis after another. When California Governor Pete Wilson approved criminal sentencing measure AB 971 (the "three-strikes law") in 1994, the already beleaguered county jails couldn't keep up with the deluge of inmates that followed. The legislation required anyone with two prior violent or serious felony convictions facing a third be sentenced to life in prison or a minimum of twenty-five years. In the past, repeat felons could plead for reduced sentences. Now they were incentivized to fight for their innocence in front of a judge. The repercussions for the jails were enormous. With more cases going to court, the number of pre-adjudicated defendants—particularly gang members and the violent and/or mentally ill—and those in trial or awaiting sentencing and transport to state prison skyrocketed.

Adding insult to injury, the 1994 Northridge earthquake and budget curtailments had delivered the final blows to the aged Hall of Justice jail and Sybil Brand Institute. Both facilities closed. In 1992, the county had broken ground between Union Station and the Los Angeles River to build a new state-of-the-art jail, the Twin Towers Correctional Facility. Four years and $373 million later, the world's largest jail was finished. Yet it stood as a monument to government inefficiency when its 4,100 beds remained empty for a year, as there was no money to run the 1.5-million-square-foot behemoth. The $100 million needed to operate Twin Towers each year was nowhere to be found. Block's hands were tied, yet he was held accountable for the debacle and ridiculed for staffing the jail with deputies to keep vagrants and vandals from breaking *in*. ACLU lawyer Peter Eliasberg came to Block's defense at the time, saying, "You can't lay it all on the sheriff. [Californians] have the will to throw people in jail, but they don't have the will to provide money so that they can live there." But Block still got the heat.

And the hits kept coming. Like rivets popping off a fatigued boiler, an onslaught of troubles in the custody division had peppered Block for the entire decade. Since filing a lawsuit against the department in 1975 over the conditions of the jails, the ACLU had continued to voice concern about the L.A. County jails. From 1991 to 1997, there had been

CHAPTER 7

150 brawls between Latino and Black inmates—in just one facility. Six murder suspects were mistakenly released while countless others were over-detained. In one case, a prisoner was held nine months past his court-ordered release date. Custody deputies were accused of encouraging inmates to beat up jailed child molesters. Inmate suicides were up, as were allegations of deputies' ugly and racist abuse of inmates. And just as Block kicked off his 1998 bid for reelection, the Department of Justice launched a special investigation into the provision of mental health services in the jails.

Despite Block's dubious record, it seemed unlikely that any of the other three contenders would collect the majority of the vote needed to unseat the incumbent in the June 2, 1998, primary. Undeterred by the old soldier's political clout and ample war chest, Lee focused on building his base and emphasizing his strengths and plans to make Los Angeles County safer and the department more effective. He spoke on the radio and television and at homeowner's groups, peace officer associations, gay and lesbian centers, and multicultural gatherings. While the city's and county's political elite called the west side and San Fernando Valley home, Lee's base came from the eastern and southern suburban middle class.

Hesitant to denigrate his friend and mentor and intent on running a clean campaign, Lee was criticized for being *too* supportive of Block's performance as sheriff. Despite Lee's maxim that "You can't hold on to your integrity when you attack someone else's," things got ugly. Block saw Lee's challenge as a personal betrayal and, worse, insubordination. And when Lee's campaign released a survey indicating voters were concerned about Block's health, the old man threw down his gloves and pounded on Lee's character and competency.

While Block had collected endorsements from Mayor Riordan, District Attorney Gil Garcetti, and the Board of Supervisors, Lee had garnered support from five contract city mayors and five city council members. The *Los Angeles Times*, however, chose not to endorse anyone during the primary, nor did ALADS or the Los Angeles County Peace Officers Association. The contest had created a bitter disruption within the department. When a commander sent a department-wide letter asking members to break ranks in favor of Lee, he was accused of inappropriate politicking and dividing the department. Sworn and non-sworn personnel were put in compromising positions and became understandably fearful of backing the wrong guy and facing repercussions later. Block continued attacking Lee, who managed to maintain his focus on the issues. He never maligned his boss, knowing how difficult Block's job was, comparing it to running a ten-ring circus.

In his campaign, Lee advocated a major shift from crisis management to preventative action through community policing. He wanted to see the department take a more active role in crime intervention and develop a stronger bond with the community through school programs, increasing literacy in the inmate population, curtailing gang activity, and eliminating bigotry through regular deputy multicultural sensitivity training. When questioned about how he would reduce inmate-on-inmate violence, Lee answered, "Training wouldn't be just a one-time shot with me . . . It would have to be on the job. You bring in a trained psychologist. You interview the fighters. Ask them why they fought. Are the brawls racial or a part of overall inmate tension?"

The electorate was divided on June 2. Block came in with 36 percent of the vote, putting Lee in second place with 32 percent. The other candidates shared the remainder. Without a majority, Block and Lee would face off in November. Amid a hundred-plus supporters on election night shouting "Viva Baca!" at the Brave Bull and Cantina in San Gabriel, Lee was filled with clattering emotions. Never a drinker and ever mindful of his family's history with alcohol, Lee raised a glass of water in the torrent of toasts. Taking in the cantina's Old West décor, he was reminded of his grandmother, Clara. Humbled by the blanket of support and enthusiasm, Lee was determined to turn the beleaguered department around and provide Los Angeles

CHAPTER 7

County residents with first-rate service. He was troubled that deputies had become divided and demoralized during the election and lamented the broken relationship with his longtime friend. He had come as far as he had in his career with Sherman Block's support. He'd have to do the rest on his own.

Three days later, Lee turned in his badge.

It was one of the most difficult decisions he had ever made. Considering how divisive the primary had been, he was concerned the schism in the department would only widen. Personnel needed to focus on their duties and couldn't afford being distracted by a virulent cocktail of office *and* civic politics. He also needed the time to focus on besting Block at the polls in November.

Lee stuck to a clean campaign—so much so that the media didn't know what to make of him. When he said the department was "in good hands now and will be in the future one way or the other," they speculated about his will to win. When asked why he didn't counter Block's attacks, he answered, "I don't believe it's necessary to go on attack mode to get my message across."

Block's campaign coffers filled with a steady stream of $1,000 donations from his well-heeled supporters—celebrities, corporations, and the power elite. The incumbent was generally well-liked, and donors knew what they'd be getting. As a long shot and a newcomer, Lee was considered too high a risk.

So, Lee pounded the pavement. He continued speaking to community groups, where $100 to $250 contributions from individual citizens and small business owners started adding up. From January to October 1998, his campaign raised $465,000—$132,000 more than Block's. When campaign finance reports listing each donation were released, Lee's was almost twice as long as Block's.

Polls showed the race as a dead heat. On Saturday, October 24, as KTLA-TV staff made final preparations to air a prerecorded Block/Baca debate, Sheriff Block slipped in his bathtub, needing ten stitches for a laceration on the back of his head. As he prepared to go to a fundraiser that evening, he felt dizzy and went to USC University Hospital for tests and observation. After a golf ball–sized blood clot was found deep in his brain, Block underwent four hours of brain surgery. It was a week before the election.

Lee immediately pulled radio ads referring to Block's age and poor health, and he cancelled all his upcoming campaign events. While Block remained in serious condition and was unable to speak, US Senator Dianne Feinstein and Mayor Riordan publicly campaigned for his reelection. Though rumors spread of Block's dire physical and mental state, the sheriff's ardent supporters escalated their efforts for his reelection.

Three days after the surgery, Block succumbed to a massive brain hemorrhage and died.

Shaken by the news, Lee released a statement: "Sherman Block was a giant in the law enforcement family . . . His dedication and commitment to his profession were unparalleled." Privately, he mourned the loss of his friend, mentor, and recent adversary.

The next few days were surreal and macabre as Block's team campaigned harder than ever . . . on behalf of a dead candidate. The thinking was that if Block prevailed, the Board of Supervisors—which had endorsed the incumbent and was responsible for selecting the next sheriff—would appoint someone from Block's camp. Lee knew whoever the board placed in office would be beholden to his kingmakers to the detriment of the department and the county.

The dissension in the department was so bitter that Block die-hards asked Baca to refrain from attending the sheriff's funeral. Lee rebuffed their petty incivility and sat quietly at the back of the Hollywood Bowl service in a show of respect for Block's family, whom he considered dear friends. He somberly hugged those he knew.

Before Block's death, polls had showed Lee ahead by 3 percent.

CHAPTER 7

Two days after the funeral, Lee won 61 percent of the vote, becoming the twenty-fifth sheriff in the LASD's near 150-year history. He was sworn in by Peter Pitchess on December 7, 1998. His son, David, by then a deputy in the department, pinned the sheriff's star to his starched uniform.

Chapter 8

Trust

"The number-one issue regarding twenty-first-century policing is not superior technology, radio car efficiency, nor command and control, all of which are important; it is simply the point of public trust."

In their first report after Lee took office, Special Counsel Merrick Bobb and staff stated,

> Sheriff Baca has lots of ideas about the job and where the sheriff's department should go. But more striking even than the flowering of many ideas, we see a very different style and approach from that of his predecessor; much greater openness, accessibility, and cards not clamped as tightly to the vest. There is a willingness—even an unrestrained eagerness to propose and embrace novel ideas, change, and unorthodox ways of doing things.

Lee's management style and philosophies on law enforcement were so different from his predecessor's that growing pains were inevitable. Block loyalists weren't sure where they stood with the new administration or if they could buy into Lee's unconventional ideas about policing. In a 2015 piece about Lee in *Los Angeles Magazine*, Celeste Fremon, founder of the blog WitnessLA and the *California Justice Report*, wrote, "Baca was seen as a big-picture man and a dreamer; more conservative members of the rank and file secretly called him 'Sheriff Moonbeam.'" Lee, of course, knew about the nickname. It didn't bother him. He actually embraced the moniker.

After the divisive election, some of the bitter old guard chose retirement over compromise and a new beginning. Lee understood that healing—or in some cases, triage—was necessary to lift morale within the department and also with the public. And he had a plan.

In a 1982 article in *The Atlantic*, James Q. Wilson and George L. Kelling wrote, "At the community level, disorder and crime are usually inextricably linked, in a kind of developmental sequence. Social psychologists and police officers tend to agree that if a window in a building is broken and is left unrepaired, all the rest of the windows will soon be broken. . . . One unrepaired broken window is a signal that no one cares."

"Broken-window policing" is a practice in which law enforcement pays more heed to seemingly small offenses such as loitering, vandalism, and littering. The theory is that a clean and orderly neighborhood sends an indirect signal to miscreants that someone is watching, reducing the likelihood of more serious crime.

In accordance with broken-window policing, Lee developed a practical guide called *Public Trust Policing: Partnering with the Communities We Protect*, stating,

> Public Trust Policing is the use of police resources in a

CHAPTER 8

manner that includes the public's participation in the mission of public safety. The purpose of Public Trust Policing is to provide a higher level of public safety. It is incumbent upon law enforcement to recognize that without the full faith and cooperation of the public, the mission of public safety is severely impaired. The process of Public Trust Policing involves moving from what was generally known as a closed system to an inclusive and open system of public participation in the public safety mission.

Lee's Public Trust Policing was based on five principles:

1. Developing methods of public participation.

2. Modeling the department's core values internally and to the public.

3. Training and supporting all department employees to be leaders.

4. Supporting college or university achievement for all law enforcement employees.

5. Creating a culture of transparency.

To encourage the public's participation, Lee formed civilian advisory committees whose members were chosen to best represent the diversity of each community. A deputy was assigned to actively participate with each group. The LASD Community-Oriented Policing Services (COPS) Bureau organized Neighborhood Watch meetings, provided services to the homeless, and as Lee had instituted in West Hollywood, conducted door-to-door surveys to determine specific local needs and concerns. Citizens were also invited to become uniformed volunteers and help with traffic control and other nonhazardous duties.

Building trust with the next generation was crucial. By 2011, approximately twenty thousand children a year participated in the Youth Activities Leagues afterschool program. Deputies reached over a hundred thousand more through the Success Through Awareness and Resistance (STAR) program, visiting 370 schools each year to promote drug, gang, and violence prevention.

The second principle of Public Trust Policing called for a written set of core values. The department's guide described it as a simple way for law enforcement agencies to define their "allegiance to the American people, their Constitution, Bill of Rights, civil rights, and human rights." It was important that the public knew what to expect from the police, and to maintain the public's trust, it was imperative that each deputy upheld the department's core values whether in or out of uniform.

One of Lee's first acts as sheriff had been to update the department's core values statement to:

> As a *leader* in the Los Angeles County Sheriff's Department, I commit myself to *honorably* perform my duties with *respect* for the dignity of all people, the *integrity* to do what is right and fight what is wrong, the *wisdom* to apply *common sense* and *fairness* in all that I do, and *courage* to stand against racism, sexism, anti-Semitism, homophobia, and bigotry in all its forms.

It was the first such creed to specifically mention anti-Semitism and homophobia, leaving no doubt where the new sheriff stood. Lee's core values statement became ubiquitous. Academy applicants needed to define what the creed meant to them. Personnel had to memorize

CHAPTER 8

it, which wasn't difficult, because it was recited often and prominently displayed in each station and jail and on all departmental publications. Lee himself recited it regularly in interviews.

Lee hoped the third principle of Public Trust Policing—training and supporting all employees to become leaders would not only foster personal and professional growth, but would also reduce or even eliminate misconduct. Explaining his philosophy, Lee said, "I'm not one to tell someone how to do something. I would only encourage someone to *try* to do something." As an example, he gave patrol station and community sheriff's station commanders "full discretion to implement participation programs of all types, depending on the needs of the communities they serve."

Lee was a scholar of leadership and management philosophy. In addition to his master's and doctorate programs, he had read extensively on the subject and through his own successes and failures as a leader had come to these conclusions:

- The first act of leadership is to love life.
- The second act of leadership is to appreciate how fragile life is.
- The third act of leadership is to live life in a thoughtful way.
- The fourth act of leadership is to conquer subjectivity with objective rationality.
- The fifth act of leadership is to live life in a courageous and giving way.

In *Deputy and Court Officer* magazine, Lee was quoted saying, "For leaders at all levels of the organization to demonstrate true leadership they need three key elements: high standards, best efforts, and noble thoughts." The sheriff believed strong, defined ethics are enhanced by improved leadership skills and that all sworn personnel would benefit from leadership training.

With this in mind, Lee created a program called the Deputy

Leadership Institute. Despite the name, it was open to everyone in the department—not just deputies—as a two-day class or a six-month college-accredited course that met three days a month.

Lee was intolerant of any deputy who abused their position. At the same time, he didn't have confidence in the efficacy of traditional disciplinary procedures. In the department's modern era, every disciplinary decision went through a complicated and lengthy review by different officers, committees, and divisions and was subject to further audits by the deputies' union and the Civil Service Commission. Typically, culpable deputies were taken off duty without pay for a number of days, the length determined by the severity of the violation. Lee had two problems with this: 1) it unfairly penalized the deputies' families financially, and 2) opportunities—teachable moments—to address deputies' transgressions through understanding and retraining were lost. The punished deputies would come back to work embittered about their loss of pay and none the wiser.

Looking for a better solution, Lee created the Education Based-Discipline (EBD) Program as an alternative to one- to thirty-day suspensions without pay. When deputies opted for EBD, they would report for duty and earn their salary. However, rather than reporting to custody, patrol, or the courthouse, they would spend a predetermined number of hours in a classroom completing an individualized remedial plan. Classes included Ethical Decision Making, Anger Management and Effective Communication, and Cultural Diversity, as well as special weapons training and specialized driving classes at the Emergency Vehicle Operation Center. Other options included assigned reading (*The 7 Habits of Highly Effective People* by Stephen R. Covey was one of the more widely read books) or briefing their peers on their area of misconduct and how they violated LASD policies.

Lee was invited to talk about EBD at the Tenth Annual Police Union Leadership Seminar at Harvard Law School in April 2009.

CHAPTER 8

Offering education as an alternative to punitive discipline had never been done in any law enforcement agency. The law enforcement officers, police union representatives, and academics in attendance were intrigued. Their interest was such that the department created a website for other agencies to request information and learn more about EBD. Lee was invited to present on the subject across the country.

As the head of the most prominent sheriff's department in the world, Lee was keen that the department be a leader too. In cooperation with the Department of Justice's COPS, the LASD's Regional Community Policing Institute extended training and technical assistance to approximately four hundred law enforcement agencies, local governments, and communities. They hosted seminars on subjects such as school violence, disaster preparedness, counterterrorism prevention, and, of course, leadership development.

As it had done before he was elected, the Merrick Bobb committee praised Lee "for his continued commitment to this training in the face of the frequent complaints we heard about these so-called 'soft skills' mandates, based not necessarily on the content of the courses but on the perception that other, more important training suffers as a result of these requirements."

In *Public Trust Policing*, Lee wrote:

> Policing in the 21st Century requires today's law enforcement official to be a versatile thinker, performer and citizen. This primary reality is driven by the complexity of modern society and the complicated issues crime creates. There is no single solution to solving today's crime problems. The only factor that is constant is that human beings will always be involved, either as a victim or perpetrator. Education is the cornerstone in successfully responding to the multi-faceted, intricate demands of modern public safety.

The fourth tenet of Public Trust Policing was education. Concurring with respected law enforcement scholar August Vollmer, Lee wanted all his deputies to have a college degree. He knew well how one's circumstances could limit life choices. College was expensive and in some families not even a consideration—overshadowed by more pressing needs like food and shelter. As one ages, family and workplace demands can leave no room for even a spark of interest. But Lee deeply believed education should be a lifelong process and in his words, "a highly educated workforce is necessary to carry out the responsibilities entrusted to us by the public we serve."

Brainstorming, jotting notes on napkins at functions as ideas streamed into his head, and dictating thoughts over the phone to one of his secretaries from his car, Lee came up with a concept that had never been tried before. He called it the Los Angeles Sheriff's Department University, or LASDU. In 2001, the department's career resources unit partnered with California State University at Long Beach to create the first law enforcement corporate university in the nation. Soon, other colleges and universities joined, including more California State universities, University of California schools, and private institutions such as Pepperdine University and Lee's alma mater, the University of Southern California. With the explosion of online learning, more colleges around the country joined in. The schools offered flexible plans to accommodate their working students and discounts such as 40-percent tuition reductions, no registration fees, and free textbooks. Though developed for LASD personnel, within a few years, enrollment opened up to any city, county, state, or federal employee, as well as to others who worked for public-service organizations *and* their immediate families.

At top universities, LASDU students could study an array of topics relevant to policing, from leadership to criminal justice, political science, forensics, health sciences, and psychology. LASD personnel leapt at the opportunity. In the program's first nine years, students

CHAPTER 8

earned over 1,500 diplomas, including 498 associate's, 789 bachelor's, 308 master's, ten PhD, and two Juris Doctor degrees.

The last, but certainly not the least, of the five principles in Lee's Public Trust Policing program was transparency. Since his days as a captain bringing citizens and deputies together to air their grievances, Lee had always looked for ways to bridge the divide between law enforcement and the public. The riots that followed the acquittal of the officers charged with beating Rodney King showed that racial tension between people of color and the police had changed little since the Zoot Suit and Watts riots—and had even worsened. Assumptions and distrust about codes of silence around police internal investigations into excessive uses of force and civilian shootings were widespread. When officers were acquitted in high-profile court cases, many believed they were literally getting away with murder.

When Lee took office, Merrick Bobb had been directing a staff of over twenty in a five-year probe into allegations against the LASD for uses of excessive force and the citizens' complaint process. Bobb had since established the nonprofit Police Assessment Resource Center (PARC) to manage the audits. By the time Lee retired, Bobb had issued thirty-four semiannual reports, generous in their praise and unvarnished in their criticisms.

Critics routinely fault law enforcement—and the LASD in particular—for its systemic lack of transparency and secrecy about internal investigations, accountability, and discipline. As the expression goes, "The police can't police themselves."

During his first term Lee did the unthinkable. In a move considered historic and precedent-setting, Lee petitioned the Board of Supervisors to fund a civilian oversight commission—the Office of Independent Review (OIR)—to be comprised of six civil attorneys with strong civil rights backgrounds and a panel of retired judges to supervise the department's Office of Internal Affairs, which investigates allegations of workplace misconduct. The OIR would also monitor the Office of Internal Criminal Investigations, which looks into cases involving corruption, excessive use of force, and other criminal acts. The commission would have complete access to all internal documents, records, and even witnesses, and would make recommendations on discipline and prosecution directly to the new sheriff. In an interview with the *Los Angeles Business Journal*, Lee said, "We need to know if we are obeying constitutional law and if we are following our own policies. If we're not doing these things, how are we self-correcting? This is a credibility challenge here that law enforcement bodies across the country face."

Dissenting deputies and management pushed back, feeling that outsiders could never fully appreciate the pressures they faced on the streets and in the jails, and that they would be unfairly judged and punished. Lee listened to their complaints but didn't waver.

The board approved Lee's $1.07 million proposal which meant the sheriff would be accountable to two separate outside entities. Bobb's fourteenth semiannual report stated, "Sheriff Baca has set an important and praiseworthy precedent by holding weekly meetings with Mike Gennaco [Chief Attorney of the Office of Independent Review for Los Angeles County], thereby giving the head of OIR unfettered access in order to communicate recommendations directly." Civil rights groups and the media cautiously welcomed this extraordinary reform, which was a stark contrast to Sherman Block's general defensiveness and reticence to expose the department's inner workings to outsiders.

From October 2002 to December 2013, the OIR published annual reports with in-depth examinations of officer-involved shootings, uses of significant force, inmate care, policy, deputy misconduct, and much more. Each (except the first) ended with appendices that identified systemic problems, the OIR's recommended solutions, and whether or not the department had implemented the commission's suggestions. An examination of these appendices substantiates Lee's willingness to

CHAPTER 8

accept criticism and documents many of the significant reforms he made as sheriff, even under tight budget and staffing constraints.

Both PARC and the OIR had Lee's ear and full access to department files and current investigations within the department. Aware that subordinates don't like to share bad news with their boss, Lee hoped these added layers of due diligence would ensure nothing escaped his attention.

In addition to OIR and PARC, the county appointed an ombudsman to investigate public complaints about officer misconduct in the sheriff's department, paying particular attention to completed service reviews and investigations that complainants found unsatisfactory. The list of agencies that had their eyes on the LASD also included the Civil Grand Jury, charged with protecting citizens from governmental abuse; the Criminal Grand Jury, which decides whether to proceed with criminal charges against deputies and a Superior Court trial; the Coroner's Department, which investigates sudden, violent, and unusual deaths; the District Attorney Office's Officer-Involved Shooting Response Program for officer/deputy-involved shootings and in-custody deaths; and the Equity Oversight Panel, which monitors charges of harassment, discrimination, and retaliation within the workplace.

To actively engage the public and garner their trust, Lee encouraged the creation of more community partnerships and volunteer programs. Citizens could attend an eight-week community academy and take classes on criminal law and patrol procedures, and even tour the Weapons Training Center and the Emergency Operations Bureau. Patrol ride-alongs and jail tours were also made available, and a direct phone line to the Internal Affairs Bureau was created to make it easier for citizens to file both complaints and commendations.

Widespread internet access and the explosion of social media further opened the lines of communication between the LASD and the public. Through apps and sites such as Nixle, Twitter, Facebook, and YouTube, users could receive up-to-the-minute information on arrests, neighborhood-specific alerts and advisories, traffic incidents, road closures, wanted persons, missing persons, and crime trends. Citizens could pose questions and comments, spurring a valuable dialogue. Email and texting made a convenient two-way system where the department could issue emergency alerts and citizens could anonymously report crimes.

Public Trust Policing worked. From 2005 to 2010, homicides in the Florence/Firestone area of South Los Angeles dropped by 72 percent and firearms-related assaults dropped by 69 percent. In 2011, the International Association of Chiefs of Police recognized Century Station with the James Q. Wilson Award for Excellence in Community Policing for the success of its public-trust policing project.

In 1998, the year before Lee was sworn in as sheriff, there were 251 homicides in Los Angeles County. In 2014, his last year in office, there were 152.

Lee knew the LASD had been hamstrung by Block's inability (or perhaps disinterest) in looking ahead and planning for the future, but he didn't realize the extent of the inefficiency until he conducted a massive audit of the organization. During his first two and a half months in office, he visited each jail and command unit, as well as all the courthouses and administrative facilities. Approachable and inquisitive, he solicited unvarnished opinions—both favorable and critical—from everyone he met to ascertain what was and wasn't working. It took seven hundred pages to list every area of concern in the final report; subjects ranged from dilapidated facilities to discriminatory promotion practices to broken copy machines.

It would be unfair to put all the blame on Block. When Californians limited real estate taxes with the passage of Proposition 13 in 1978, government-funded agencies took a big hit. A budget crisis

CHAPTER 8

from 1993 to 1996 kept Los Angeles County on the verge of bankruptcy and it cut back spending across the board. To make matters worse, the state then diverted billions from local governments to quell its own financial crisis. In the subsequent years-long hiring freeze, the department lost six hundred deputies.

After his departmental audit, Lee began tackling the laundry list of problems. He worked with four of his commanders to develop a thirty-year strategic plan dubbed LASD2. Together they proposed seventy-three projects "to improve service excellence, children and families' well-being, workforce excellence, fiscal integrity, and facilities planning." Action plans included building new stations and upgrading the old and improving educational programs for both personnel and inmates. About LASD2, Lee said, "I'm being creative with the bureaucracy instead of being confined by it. . . . We're making dynamic changes."

Lee's ambitious vision came with a hefty price tag—an estimated $1 billion over a thirty-year period—at a time when money was scarce. After the 9/11 attacks, voters had approved a property tax increase to help subsidize the county's trauma system. Encouraged by the public's sacrifice, Lee proposed the Board of Supervisors create a ballot measure to increase the county sales tax by half a cent in 2002, allocating the expected $500 million generated annually to the department to carry forth his proposed plan. The Board of Supervisors unanimously rejected Lee's idea. He pitched them again and was shut down a second time. Undeterred, Lee went around the board and campaigned to collect the two hundred thousand signatures required to put the measure on the November 2004 ballot. Lee explained his strategy: "I used my political influence that I've knitted quietly, under the radar screen. . . . How did this all happen? It was an army of ants. I pay attention to the people many others don't notice." Despite support from his growing and diverse fan base, as well as then LAPD Chief Bill Bratton and oddly enough, rapper Won-G, the campaign fell short of its goal.

During this time, the department and its new head were lambasted for a series of grievous incidents in the custody division. Overcrowding in the jails had reached a critical point. There just wasn't enough space or staff to provide the necessary security and basic care. After a 2002 budget showdown, the Board of Supervisors withdrew funding for the seven-year-old Century Regional Detention Facility (CRDF) in Lynwood and forced its closure, displacing 1,600 inmates and leaving Lee to pick up the pieces.

After the expected domino effect stressed the entire system, Lee made the grim decision to release thousands of low-level offenders—those whose bail was under $25,000 and who weren't charged with violent crimes or crimes against children—before their sentences were completed. The public outcry was immediate. Then, when five inmates were killed by fellow inmates between October 2003 and April 2004, the ACLU, US DOJ, media, and special interest groups demanded answers and change. Families of the deceased sued the department, seeking millions in damages.

Resolute that life—*every* life—is a gift, Lee was anguished about the homicides that had occurred on his watch. He welcomed teams from internal and external agencies to dissect each case to pinpoint failures in policy and deputies' failures to follow policy. Those deputies needed to be identified and held accountable. In further testament to his commitment to transparency, Lee even invited the media into the jails to which they had little to no access in the past. While his predecessors had been accused of secrecy, Lee wanted to prove he had nothing to hide.

Adding to the troubles of 2003, hundreds of deputies came down with the "blue flu" that fall. The deputies' union and the county had reached a stalemate in contract negotiations over a 3-percent salary increase and improvement in benefits. The initial wildcat strikes that had shut down courthouses spread to patrol stations. On one day, all twenty-five deputies assigned to one station's day shift called in sick.

CHAPTER 8

Lee understood their anger but could not abide the consequential risk to public safety. A Superior Court judge had declared the walkout illegal, and Lee made it clear he would have no problem jailing his own deputies for contempt of court. Luckily, it didn't come to that and the union and county reached an agreement.

The Board of Supervisors had initially declined to support Lee's sales tax proposal in part because they thought he was exaggerating the extent of his problems. But their case weakened with each hit to the department. From a risk-management standpoint (their mandate to ensure the safety of all citizens aside), the legal fees, settlements, and payouts from lawsuits filed against the LASD were untenable. They pivoted on the half-cent tax initiative and put the measure on the November 2004 ballot. It didn't pass.

The board eventually unearthed more money for the department, and Lee continued to appeal to LASD contract cities, the state capitol, and federal agencies—such as the US Department of Justice, the Office of Community Oriented Policing Services (COPS), and the Federal Emergency Management Agency (FEMA)—for more.

When Lee was elected, he and Carol Chiang had been dating for a couple years. The Taiwanese-born beauty had played a big role in Lee's campaign. They had met at a social function, and it was at another that he took her completely by surprise. Somewhat of a celebrity by then, Lee was Carol's guest at an alumni gathering for her high school when he was asked to take the microphone and give a speech. After saying a few words, he concluded by announcing that he and Carol were getting married. No one in the room was more surprised than Carol.

Anticipating the avalanche of demands on his time, the new sheriff wanted to say "I do" before his schedule got even crazier. In three whirlwind weeks, Lee and Carol planned their wedding, marrying on May 29, 1999.

It had been a prescient move, for after Lee became sheriff,

he needed five secretaries to manage his calendar. Social and job-related invitations came from all over the world, often conflicting or overlapping. Not wanting to let anyone down, Lee accepted almost every invitation. On some evenings the couple went from one event to another to another, sometimes being served multiple meals a night. But just as likely, the timing was such that they'd miss out on food altogether. As others pulled Lee from their table, Carol would often find the seat next to her empty. But she appreciated the opportunity it gave her to meet so many interesting people. Whether her husband was mingling with heads of state, religious leaders, victims of crimes, or community activists, Carol could easily find him in the crowd. His clean dome supported by his six-foot-one frame always gave him away.

Lee's list of daily engagements was so varied, he sometimes changed his clothes more than four times a day. Predictably, he started each day in running gear. But after that, he could switch between his khaki uniform, jeans and a T-shirt, a suit, or a tuxedo. Leading the country's largest sheriff's department required Lee to continually pivot from one role to another, whether it be as politician, fundraiser, mentor, disciplinarian, spokesperson, or volunteer. Yet above all, Lee saw himself as a social worker. Reforming the community through outreach and education and building trust were the cornerstone of every effort.

To best serve the public, it was incumbent on Lee that his facilities kept up with changes in technology and the county's increasing population. Aging infrastructure needed to be improved or replaced.

For example, when San Dimas Station was built on half an acre at the easternmost area of LASD's jurisdiction in 1950, the area's population was 1,840. In 2005, its population of 35,421 was served by big box stores, national grocery chains, the largest water park on the West Coast, and the same 1950 sheriff's station. The city of San Dimas donated a four-acre lot to the county for a new station. In homage to the old station, blueprints included a brick façade but with

CHAPTER 8

a more modern flair. Wide steps led to an entrance shaded by an angled roof, a lobby with hunter green accents, and an inviting welcome area with a polished granite counter. In accordance with Lee's vision, the new station included a community room for public meetings, as well as a learning center with high-speed internet and computers for LASDU students.

After a weeklong assessment of the new facility in 2007, a Netherlands-based group, whose mission was to improve public safety and justice internationally, named the San Dimas Station the highest-rated police station in North America with its Altus Global Alliance Award. In its decision, the group cited the station's community orientation, detention conditions, transparency, and accountability.

Opened in 1992 in the Mojave Desert with a staff of forty, Palmdale Station had started out as a substation of Antelope Valley Sheriff's Station. It occupied a storefront office space at first but expanded as the community grew. A fully independent station by 1998 (no longer a substation), the facility had more than doubled in size to 13,500 square feet but still lacked a jail, secure parking, gas pumps, and a heliport. It couldn't provide the level of service to which Lee aspired, so he approved plans to update the station. In the spring of 2006, four hundred personnel moved into new digs on a roughly eleven-acre parcel. In the corridors of the 47,000-square-foot terracotta tile–roofed building, staff no longer needed to turn sideways when passing each other.

Since Lennox Station had first opened in 1948 between Los Angeles International Airport and the Hollywood Park Racetrack, its geographical jurisdiction had slowly decreased with the opening of the Lomita, Carson, and Marina del Rey stations. But the population had continued to increase within its narrower boundaries, so the station was beyond obsolete. In 2010, under Lee's guidance, just north of Interstate 105, a $24 million station with a new name—South Los Angeles Station—replaced Lennox. Reminiscent of California's early missions, an arched stone arcade created a friendly and welcome atmosphere. Like San Dimas Station, it included a community room and learning center. The station also boasted a state-of-the-art computer-aided dispatch center, a thirty-seven-bed jail, and an emergency operations center to better manage crisis situations.

When England's House of Commons Chamber had to be replaced after it was destroyed in the Blitz in 1940, members of Parliament petitioned for the more open, modern semicircular design being adopted by other countries. Winston Churchill opposed the plan, successfully advocating the new chamber be built to recreate the room's cramped, rectangular shape. He argued the confined space fostered debate, squeezing the two parties together, making them more likely to be confrontational. In a 1943 speech to Parliament, he said, "We shape our buildings; thereafter they shape us."

Appreciating the immeasurable effects architecture and design can have on the human psyche, Lee insisted the new stations not be depressing government-gray bureaucratic clichés. In our subconscious, colors, lighting, open design, and feng shui can raise and lower our emotions and sense of trust. Understanding that most citizens enter a sheriff's station under negative circumstances, feeling uncomfortable, intimidated, scared, or angry (and often all four at once), Lee wanted to make the experience as pleasant as possible. He took an active role in the design of each new station, from floor plans to choosing tile. It was all part of his effort to create an environment where the public felt welcomed, and where the staff were happier to work.

But Lee had ideas grander than merely replacing decrepit stations. He was changing the Los Angeles landscape and the Hall of Justice was central to his vision.

At the corner of downtown's Temple and Broadway Streets, the Hall of Justice was built in 1925 to house the county's sheriff's department, coroner, district attorney, public defender, and tax collector. Conveniently catercorner from city hall, the fourteen-story building

CHAPTER 8

had seventeen courtrooms and a 750-cell jail—and if those walls could talk . . . Bugsy Siegel, Evel Knievel, and Robert Mitchum had been incarcerated there over the years. And some of the city's grimmest moments had transpired in the imposing structure—the Sleepy Lagoon, Sirhan Sirhan, and Charles Manson trials, as well as Robert F. Kennedy's and Marilyn Monroe's autopsies.

Minutes from Hollywood, the beaux arts building was a regular location for television dramas *Perry Mason*, *Get Smart*, and *Dragnet*.

The Hall of Justice had persisted after a bombing by a radical group in the seventies, an accidental fire fueled by confiscated cannabis and cocaine in the eighties, and society's worst for almost seven decades, but was no match for Father Time or Mother Nature. Starting in 1971, tenants packed up one by one and left the decaying edifice for more modern and comfortable offices. The sheriff's department was one of the last to abandon ship when Sherman Block relocated LASD headquarters to a leased five-story Monterey Park office building in 1993. The twelve-acre property held great potential for expansion and was adjacent to the Sybil Brand Institute and the department's original training center.

Nine months after the department moved to Monterey Park, the 6.7-magnitude Northridge earthquake rocked the city, delivering the Hall of Justice's final blow. It was red-tagged, and Civic Center pigeons and vermin were given an all-access pass to the once-glorious grande dame.

Lee had never forgotten reporting to the Hall of Justice for his first day of work in 1965. The grandeur and sheer bulk of the landmark building had evoked an almost sacred feeling inside the young trainee. Its solemn representation of law and order and the gravity of its occupants' responsibilities and duties were unambiguous. While Lee wanted stations to feel welcoming and open, he felt the department's headquarters should evoke humility, awe, and respect—qualities the Monterey Park office sorely lacked. Before the LASD took over the lease, the building had housed a fiberglass, concrete, and steel pipe manufacturer. While the space was serviceable, it was generic and designed for corporate tenants.

And so began Lee's efforts to save the Hall of Justice, so his department could "go home." Others had tried and failed, but once the Board of Supervisors gave him the green light, Lee spearheaded a successful fundraising drive for the Hall of Justice Repair and Reuse Project. After considering the annual $8.5 million it would save when leased office spaces were off the books, the county released funds from its capital projects budget. FEMA issued the county a $16 million grant, which covered less than half of the seismic retrofitting costs from damage sustained by the Northridge earthquake. Once all avenues of federal and state funding had been exhausted, Lee worked to create a public/private partnership.

Two decades and $231 million after the catastrophic earthquake, the hall's stately bronze entry doors opened for the sheriff's department and district attorney office's homecoming in 2014. By that time, Lee had retired. He attended the ribbon-cutting ceremony and saw his successor was among the list of names engraved on the bronze dedication plaque. It may come as a surprise that the slight didn't bother Lee. Results had always been more important to him than accolades. He nodded when speakers heralded his role in saving the building and, according to the *Los Angeles Times*, "accepted a hug from just about everyone who passed." Though his name wasn't on the building, his fingerprints were all over it in the small details he had pressed for: the green paint on the windows (an homage to its sister building, the city hall), the translucent panels that brought light from adjacent hallways to previously dark spaces, and more. The building was LEED Gold certified for its use of environmentally friendly materials and won multiple awards for its design, construction, and historical preservation.

CHAPTER 8

★ ★ ★ ★ ★

Richard Buckland was the first person in the world exonerated by DNA evidence. In 1986, the seventeen-year-old boy with learning disabilities had admitted to raping and murdering a schoolgirl in Leicestershire, England. He later retracted his confession only to once more confess, retract, and confess in a confusing cycle. Two years prior, geneticist Alec Jeffreys had accidentally discovered unique and identifying patterns in DNA in his lab at the nearby university while studying inherited diseases. His breakthrough had been used to solve cases involving immigration and paternity and for identifying twins. At Jeffreys's first public talk about his findings, he proposed that DNA fingerprinting could be used to solve crimes. His idea seemed so far-fetched that some audience members couldn't stifle their laughter. But the local police in attendance didn't laugh. Instead, they sought his help in the Buckland investigation.

After serving three months in custody, Buckland was cleared of the rape and murder. The DNA from the crime scene had been matched to another murder Buckland couldn't have committed. In a controversial dragnet, the police had collected blood samples from over 5,500 local men. They caught the murderer after his friend told pub mates he had falsely submitted his own blood sample to protect his friend.

Forensic science had taken a leap that Sir Arthur Conan Doyle could not have imagined. By the mid-1990s, DNA evidence was admissible in most US courtrooms, including those in California. Equipment manufacturers, researchers, and police departments scrambled to keep apace with the new technology.

In 1994, when LASD Scientific Services Bureau (SSB) crime lab director Barry Fisher heard the University of California, Riverside, was discussing building a new crime lab with the DOJ, he had an idea. After all, California State University, Los Angeles, had one of the longest-running graduate programs in criminal justice and criminalistics in the country and was literally a stone's throw from LASD headquarters.

Crime labs throughout the country recruited recent graduates from CSULA and for the school to share a facility with a department as large as the LASD seemed like a win-win for everyone.

A few years later, the Los Angeles County Grand Jury examined the city's and county's crime labs and concluded what insiders already knew: they were undersized and understaffed; the equipment, antiquated. Distinguished for having the country's first crime lab in 1923—even before the FBI—the LAPD's bureau had taken a deep dive since its glory days. In the O. J. Simpson murder trial, defense attorneys lambasted the lab's substandard performance. Space was so inadequate, its serology unit had spilled into the administration building's cafeteria.

On the county level, the LASD's SSB—which included sections for forensic biology, narcotics, polygraph, toxicology, and special units such as photo/digital imaging, evidence control, and information systems—was housed in five labs spread over an eighty-mile swath. The Grand Jury recommended LAPD and LASD consolidate their testing sites to cut costs.

By the time Lee became sheriff, plans were already underway to build a joint-agency crime lab for the LAPD, LASD, and the CSULA School of Criminal Justice and Criminalistics. The first assessment had concluded that meeting all three institutions' needs required a 320,000-square-foot building. But the attendant $132 million price tag was prohibitive. Voters had rejected a $220 million bond measure to fund a new building in 1999. Lee pressed on and enlisted the clout of democrats Robert Hertzberg (the Speaker of the California Assembly) and State Senator Richard Polanco. Thanks to their vision and persistence, Governor Gray Davis appropriated $96 million—enough to build a 209,080-square-foot lab. The LASD was chosen as the lead agency of the Los Angeles Regional Crime Laboratory Facility Authority—a joint powers authority formed in 2001.

The idea was that by sharing testing equipment, evidence storage

CHAPTER 8

rooms, vehicle processing areas, and a firing range, the LASD and LAPD would save the county and the city money. But as is the case with any bureaucratic endeavor, what seemed like a sensible plan led to interagency discord and protracted negotiations. Each department had different needs, and at the outset the only thing Lee and LAPD Chief Bernard Parks could agree on was that they each wanted to control their own operations. The project's facilitator worked to find consensus. For the project to succeed, there had to be a single vision. Lee had expected they would share some technology and staff, but Parks was completely opposed. Ongoing disagreements delayed construction and jeopardized funding, but they eventually reached a compromise that 25 percent of what would be known as the Hertzberg-Davis Forensic Science Center (after Lee rebutted calls that the building bear his name) would be shared space.

The entire second floor was occupied by CSULA laboratories, offices, student work areas, a computer lab, a library, and four large multimedia lecture rooms. The university had turned Lee's life around and he was grateful to be in a position where he could pay it back and forward at the same time. Like himself, most students at his alma mater were Latinos and the first in their families to attend college. Ever mindful of the powerful influence of one's environment, Lee knew the proximity to an active, modern crime lab would energize and inspire students. Immersed in the real-world culture—with working criminalists for professors and guest lecturers—graduate students had access to internships and an inside advantage when looking for employment. CSULA President James M. Rosser enthused that the collaborations created between faculty, students, and working criminalists would "bridge the gap between scientific advancements and their effective use in crime laboratories."

The crime lab was the second largest in the United States—second only to the FBI's in Quantico, Virginia. Besides the LASD and LAPD, forty-six other police agencies and the district and city attorneys' offices benefitted from the available services. The Hertzberg-Davis Forensic Science Center also became home to the newly formed California Forensic Science Institute (CFSI). CFSI provided support for research and career development and was a hub for information on national and international forensics meetings. Before opening day in 2007, Elizabeth Devine—who had received a master of science degree in criminalistics from CSULA and worked for LASD before becoming a producer on *CSI: Crime Scene Investigation*—presented a $25,000 check to the institute. After all, this was L.A.

When a Los Angeles city/county joint crime lab was first proposed, the use of DNA fingerprinting was still in its infancy. But by the time the center opened in 2007, the LAPD and LASD had amassed an ungodly amount of evidence that sat untested in storage facilities. In 2009, Human Rights Watch (HRW) published "Testing Justice: The Rape Kit Backlog in Los Angeles City and County." The logjam of untested rape kits was a national problem, but after visiting LASD and LAPD crime labs and evidence storage facilities and conducting 130 interviews from police executives and crime lab personnel to rape survivors themselves, researchers concluded that the city and county of Los Angeles—with 12,669 untested kits between them—had the dubious honor of having the country's largest stockpile.

HRW wrote:

> The police department, in particular, has struggled to expeditiously tackle its rape kit backlog, its efforts complicated by city politics, battles over crime lab funding, and changes in internal leadership over the issue. It is essential that county and city leaders, both within and outside of law enforcement, move quickly to test every rape kit in the county. Eliminating delays in rape kit testing is especially crucial to realizing justice for rape victims in California, where the ten-year statute

CHAPTER 8

of limitations (the maximum time period after a crime when a defendant may be prosecuted) for rape can be lifted if the rape kit is tested within two years of the date of the crime and a DNA profile is found.

In the same report, HRW went on to say, "As of February 2009, after pressure from Human Rights Watch and other advocacy groups, the sheriff's department has counted and catalogued its untested rape kits in more detail than any other police department in the United States of which Human Rights Watch is aware." By April 2011, when all the kits had been tested, 753 had been matched in the national DNA database.

Today, about eighty DNA analysts work in the Hertzberg-Davis Forensic Science Center crime labs, processing around 230,000 cases a year. Some cases involve evidence that has been in storage for decades. One of the highest-profile cold cases the homicide division cracked during Lee's sixteen years as sheriff reached back to 1957 and the murders of two El Segundo Police Department officers.

Twenty-five-year-old Milton Curtis had been with the force for two months when he and his partner, Richard Phillips stopped a motorist for running a red light. They had no way of knowing the car was stolen and belonged to one of four teens the driver had just assaulted, bound, blindfolded, and robbed before raping one of them, a fifteen-year-old girl. The driver fatally shot each officer three times, dumped the car, and hitchhiked his way into obscurity and a new life. Despite numerous witnesses, two partial fingerprints, and the eventual recovery of the murder weapon, the cop killer remained elusive after decades of dead-end leads.

In 2000, Lee had assigned a team of five detectives to review thousands of unsolved homicides. Two years later, LASD was one of the first agencies to link into the FBI's national fingerprint database. The Integrated Automated Fingerprint Identification System (IAFIS) technology made it easy for departments to cross-reference collected fingerprints. When sheriff's detectives Kevin Lowe and Dan McElderry uploaded the fingerprints collected in 1957 from the stolen car to IAFIS, they found a match to a 1956 burglary conviction. The murderer—by now a sixty-nine-year-old respected member of his community—was arrested at his South Carolina home by El Segundo Police and Los Angeles Sheriff's officers in 2003. He pled guilty and was sentenced to two consecutive life terms. He died in prison in 2017, sixty years after taking the lives of the two police officers.

Beyond upholding justice and accountability, the resolution of a cold case can bring the victim's family an immeasurable sense of closure, and the investigators and department responsible, an equal feeling of accomplishment and honor. While no life is more valuable than another, when the victim is a peace officer, emotions are heightened. For every day they don their uniform, they know it might be their last. Not only do they put themselves at risk to protect complete strangers, but their families also silently serve alongside them, knowing the dreaded knock on the door could come at any moment. Any police chief or sheriff will tell you the worst part of the job is when someone under their command is killed in the line of duty.

Grievers are intuitive to false empathy and lip service, but in one personal account after another, Lee's authenticity and care were universally recognized. When one officer's father was in hospice, Lee spent hours by his side offering what comfort he could, even though he had never met the man. He consoled victims of crime, whomever they were. But the depth of feelings when one of his deputies was killed under his watch was profound, and holding the murderer accountable was paramount.

When thirty-three-year-old Deputy David March pulled a driver to the side of the road in April 2002, he had no idea the man behind the wheel had been deported multiple times and had bragged to friends that he planned to elicit a traffic stop that day solely so he could kill a cop. Completely exposed in front of his patrol car at approximately

CHAPTER 8

10:40 a.m., Deputy March was shot several times in the head and chest and left for dead. In his account of that tragic day, John March, David's father, wrote:

> I met Sheriff Baca on the 29 of April 2002. We had just received the news that our son, Deputy David March, had been gunned down. It was the worst day in our lives and the only light was our family and a man we had never met, Lee Baca. We were at the hospital where they brought our son's body. I drove to the hospital and the sheriff had picked my wife up in a helicopter at our home in Lake Arrowhead. The sheriff was there for us that horrible day and had his arms around us for hours. He gave us his home phone, cell phone, and private office phone number and told us to call him any time day or night. We took him up on that offer many times when life became too dark, and he always took the time to talk to us for as long as we needed his loving words.

A few years after the shooting, Lee took the words March had written on his last review and they became the department's creed: "My goals in life are simple. I will always be painfully *honest, work* as hard as I can, *learn* as much as I can, and hopefully *make a difference* in people's lives."

A person of interest had been identified immediately after Deputy March's murder, but had fled to Mexico. Lee hounded US Marshals and worked with Mexican federal agents to secure his extradition to California. For transport from the jail to the courthouse, deputies used March's handcuffs to secure the suspect. He pled guilty to the murder in 2007 and was sentenced to life in prison without the possibility of parole.

Chapter 9

A Life Worth Living

*"The uneducated mind will predictably live
in a threatened and limited way."*

Removed from mainstream society—packed into a noisy space with limited resources—adversarial gangs, violent offenders, the mentally ill, and "non, non, non" (non-serious, non-sex-related, nonviolent) inmates must learn to coexist in an environment thick with fear and hate. For some, survival means flexing their power through intimidation and physical violence. For others, it means becoming submissive and invisible, maintaining unflinching hyper-vigilance. In short, the skills one hones on the inside are antithetical to what is needed to sustain a peaceful society on the outside. As Lee succinctly said, "The values needed to succeed in jail are often in direct conflict with societal norms." Unfortunately, these prison skills become ingrained in the individual. And this is what released prisoners take back with them to mainstream society.

While the incarcerated focused on simply getting through another day, Lee saw so much wasted time, opportunity, and potential. For too many, mind-numbing TV shows and idle conversation were the sum total of their mental stimulation. Lee knew their lives could be changed for the better and in his rarefied position, he could make it happen.

In a 2011 interview he explained, "If you incarcerate the body and the mind combined, you're basically protecting society while they're in prison, but you're not doing much when they get out. Because it's the mind that is the ultimate tool of success. Ninety percent of jail inmates will get out. They have to be better prepared while they're being incarcerated to think differently about the free world and their choices."

Beginning with the Student and the Law classes he had taught as a young sergeant, education had been a constant thread throughout Lee's years in uniform, whether as a student or teacher. Steadfast in his belief that a society can't arrest its way out of crime, Lee knew education would help. Though studies concurred that educational programs played a role in reducing recidivism, in 2010, only 15 percent of the US prison population was enrolled in classes. The number was lower for municipal jails.

Arguably, education and competent life skills contribute to personal success. Statistics confirm they also reduce one's propensity toward criminal behavior and the likelihood of returning to prison. But improved education alone can't guarantee an inmate will successfully transition into society upon reentry. Though they may be more book smart, the same problems that got them into trouble in the first place lie in wait like an evil clown in a storm drain, hungry to drag them down into the abyss of social risk factors for crime.

Beyond practical schooling, new research had found two equally—perhaps even greater—contributing factors to post-release success: cognitive behavioral therapy (CBT) and post-incarceration services.

CBT helps individuals recognize the distortions in their own thought processes that can lead to emotional overreactions and misguided perceptions about themselves and the world. After identifying these patterns and triggers, the psychotherapist and patient create an action plan with new coping strategies that reduce maladaptive behaviors and lead to better outcomes. Through increased self-awareness and positive reinforcement, CBT has proven effective in treating several mental health disorders.

Educational programs in L.A. jails had come a long way since their introduction in 1913, and mirrored conventional offerings at state and federal prisons and large county jails. But as a visionary, Lee was always pushing the envelope. After working with Richard Weintraub, with whom he had developed the Student and the Law classes four decades earlier, Lee formally introduced a plan for Education Based Incarceration (EBI) in 2010. EBI incorporated education, vocational training, CBT, and post-incarceration services to deter criminal behavior and reduce recidivism by creating a supportive environment. Speaking to instructor David Belasco's class at USC in 2012, Lee said:

> I will not turn my back on the people in my jails. I will help them learn how to grow beyond where they are. That's what Education Based Incarceration is, and I'm going to transform the state prison system. . . . That's what I'm living for—transformational capabilities with human beings that have struggled with how life can be a wonderful thing. It's not fun to be in jail. It's not fun to be indicted. It's not fun to have some mental illness. It's not fun to be homeless. All that stuff is out there, and people need a law enforcement guy that has an understanding as to how they can climb out of it, and that's my mission: to help people climb out of the things that are getting in the way of their goodness.

EBI focused on three different phases of an inmate's journey: Going in, time in, and going out.

GOING IN: The Inmate Reception Center (IRC) at downtown's Twin Towers Correctional Facility is the first stop for all L.A. County inmates. The IRC processes over four hundred new bookings each day where staff determine the best placement to ensure each prisoner's safety based on their race, sexual orientation, criminal history, military service, and gang affiliation. EBI introduced a new step to the intake process to see if arrestees would be interested in participating in educational programs during their incarceration. For those interested, an individualized master plan was created factoring in the circumstances of their arrest, level of education and life skills, substance abuse history, mental health, and overall employability.

TIME IN: The average stay for non-non-nons in L.A. County jails in 2012 was fifty-four days. Given their longer court cases and reinstatement from state prison to finish their sentences, violent offenders averaged a year and a half in county jail. With such a broad range of time served, programming needed to be highly efficient and offered in long-term and short-term modules.

Financial support for existing academic programs came from the state based on average daily classroom attendance. Other programs were subsidized by federal revenue and the inmates themselves via the Inmate Welfare Fund—monies collected from payphone calls and commissary purchases. Dismissing skeptics who said there just wasn't enough money available for EBI, Lee argued that by reducing recidivism, the program would pay for itself over time.

He found creative solutions. Though some classes needed to be taught by accredited teachers, EBI could defer costs by utilizing volunteer instructors: deputies, non-sworn custody assistants, and outside citizens. Even inmates with advanced skill sets could help. IRC intake

CHAPTER 9

assessments revealed a spectrum of deficiencies. Some inmates lacked basic language and math skills and needed remedial classes before they could even begin high school studies, but most were only a course or two shy of earning their diplomas. And there were those in between: candidates for the state high school equivalency test or GED. Through its Correctional Education Program, the department had a cost-neutral contract with the Hacienda-La Puente Unified School District and later added other charter schools. The curriculum was based on the California Department of Education standards. Because most employers require a high school diploma, courses were designed for those inmates who hadn't completed their schooling and would have trouble landing jobs.

On top of helping some inmates complete their degrees, EBI supported students overcoming illiteracy, and offered an ESL program to limited- and non-English speakers. Additionally, the thousands of eighteen- to twenty-two-year-olds who received special education services through individualized education plans (IEPs) from their school districts were ensured the same opportunities while incarcerated.

The vocational training options for inmates were broad and designed so they could reach basic levels of proficiency in a short amount of time. Longer programs led to mastery, and participants in programs accredited by the California Department of Education could leave jail with a certified credential, opening doors to a previously unimagined future. Woven into the curricula were essential practical skills such as resume writing, interviewing techniques, and workplace grooming, attire, and etiquette.

As part of EBI, inmates serviced bicycles used by patrol and refurbished and then donated bikes for children. Those in the commercial sewing classes made inmate clothing, linens, and mattresses, as well as hand-sewn dolls for community organizations to distribute during the holidays. Participants in the commercial masonry and construction classes built retention walls, barbecue areas, pathways, hardscapes for sheriff's facilities, and even a World War II memorial at Pitchess Detention Center. Though the extensive farming operations at Pitchess (the former Wayside Honor Rancho) had been all but eliminated in 1992 due to budget curtailments, there was still a nursery where inmates cultivated plants, shrubs, and trees that were used for landscaping department facilities and sold to nonprofits and government agencies. Harvested vegetables and fruits were used in the culinary arts programs for inmates, in individually packaged meals for those in station holding cells, and in school lunch programs. Anything extra was donated to food-insecure communities.

Such extensive programming is available in state and federal prisons, but not so common in local jails. Of the men and women in his jails, Lee said:

> I'm not telling them that I can change them. I'm saying, "What you know will change you." It's not pounding license plates; it's not doing laundry work. Those are the traditional rehabilitation programs—put them to work, keep them busy, teach them some skills. Truth is, those are time-passing forms of work that keep the prison institution in order. I have all that. But I don't want my inmate cooks or printers thinking they're going to go out and become a cook or a printer. Some will do that, but it's such a small number.

EBI was designed to take inmates beyond the expectations of traditional custody programs which are geared to give inmates the tools they need to find a job. In the hands of someone with low emotional intelligence, those tools are often ineffective. EBI classes taught interpersonal skills and the means to build a post-release strong support system that encompassed faith, family, friends, and work. EBI offered classes to built character and dignity. There were the classes one might expect, such as substance abuse and anger management, but the curricula went deeper, encompassing critical thinking, decision-making, communication, goal-setting, positive thinking, leadership, and spiritual growth, and skills to improve parenting and personal relationships.

To critics of EBI who believed time served should be punitive and harsh, the JFA Institute, which specializes in justice and corrections research, had this to say in their 2013 "Evaluation of Education-Based Incarceration Programs Los Angeles County Sheriff's Department Jail System":

> And although some segment of the public, as well as a significant and less enlightened portion of the law enforcement community itself oppose what they would choose to regard as the *mollycoddling* or *spoiling* of inmates, it is an incontrovertible fact that people with something to lose are less likely to be sent to jail than those with nothing to lose but their freedom. Thus, employment and all that it brings with it including a more stable family environment, possible homeownership, pride about one's own accomplishments, a sense of being a productive member of the community rather than an outsider or even worse one of its victims, all serve as possibly powerful antidotes to recidivism.

One of EBI's goals was to expand the Maximizing Education Reaching Individual Transformation (MERIT) program. Because the department's budget had been cut to the bone, the program was made possible by volunteers from partnerships Lee had cultivated with community- and faith-based organizations, as well as inmate instructors who honed their own leadership skills by mentoring other inmates. To inculcate their new habits, participants ate, attended class, and even lived together in a dedicated dorm regardless of race and security level, an arrangement unheard of in traditional correctional settings. There were also dedicated tracks for US military veterans and ex-gang members. By 2013, the South Facility at Pitchess housed 1,260 participants in fourteen barracks.

MERIT remains one of Lee's enduring legacies. In the early days, inmates could request to join the program and were also recruited from the general population by MERIT graduates. But after seeing the lower recidivism rates and outside success experienced by program graduates, judges began mandating inmates' participation by court order.

The interdisciplinary program was designed on a progressive scale.

In MERIT Beginnings, basic life skills are taught by MERIT graduates over a six-week period.

MERIT Life Skills is a twelve-week series emphasizing career, commitment, and relationships. Upon completion, students can apply to the MERIT Masters Program and are selected based on oral exam performance. Those who aren't accepted into the Masters Program can opt to stay in their MERIT dorm to work on their exit plan for their reentry.

Students in the MERIT Masters Program mentor Beginnings and Life Skills students and join one of the following committees: Executive, New Member Relations, Tutoring, Marketing/Promotions, and Volunteer. Masters Graduates can stay in the MERIT dorm and teach, or choose to return to the general population to provide mentorship and recruit new students for the remainder of their sentence. Graduates can also volunteer at juvenile facilities.

MERIT Continuum is a post-release support group for former students that meets once a week at locations throughout the county.

Another of MERIT's innovative features was a family support group network that took place simultaneously on the outside. Here, in keeping with Lee's community-based approach to policing, parents, spouses, and children were offered a touchstone to what their incarcerated loved ones were working on, as well as a place to share their own pain, worries, and plans.

The effectiveness of MERIT is supported by statistics, observations, and participant testimonials. Cynics who may think MERIT was successful because participants were carefully culled from the general population should heed the JFA's observations: "EBI inmates are not 'light-weight' inmates. They are charged or convicted of serious crimes and are classified as medium custody or higher. . . . EBI participants are not some 'cherry-picked' subgroup of inmates, but contain people convicted of violent and nonviolent crimes, long and minimal prior records, and extensive drug abuse histories."

The 2013 JFA study found that in March 2013, the Pitchess South Facility's inmate-on-inmate assault rate per 100 inmates was 7.1. In the MERIT Masters dorm located in the same building, it was 1.6. An analysis of the male and female MERIT dorms at Twin Towers also found a lower assault rate than in the general population.

A year earlier, the department had published a review about EBI. At the time, California had one of the highest recidivism rates in the United States at 63 percent. The report stated, "While reviewing records of inmates who have been involved in our MERIT program, we selected a sampling of all inmates who had participated in the program over the past calendar year (September 2011 through August 2012). Out of the 1,125 inmates who had participated in the program, we found that 569 had been released from custody. Out of that number, 209 have been rearrested and convicted of new crimes. This results in a recidivism rate of 36.7 percent." Though not a definitive, empirical study, the news was encouraging, especially for such a young program.

It is impossible to completely eliminate violence in jails. How can you take someone's freedom without incurring hostility fueled by their understandable anger and resentment? While EBI was off to a promising start, changing the culture and reducing assaults between inmates and staff in an institution as overcrowded and underfunded as the L.A. County jails would take years. Lee knew that if given enough time, change would come, and the results would speak for themselves. He also knew his critics would be impatient and relentless unless he did the impossible: eliminate all violence from the jails overnight. One inmate suicide or homicide or one disgraceful deputy would make front-page headlines, and nominal but life-altering wins would remain unnoticed.

But seasoned penal workers and inspectors were astonished when they visited the MERIT dorms. The following is from an article on the Board of State and Community Corrections (BSCC) California website titled "L.A. County Jail Education Programs Transform Lives":

> Prison societies that divided inmates by ethnic background or gang affiliation have broken down as educated inmates start to see themselves as human beings first. . . . Inmates of all backgrounds work to tutor each other in classes. The tension level in the jail is reduced and inmate-officer relations have improved. "Look at that pod—you have races that are mixed. That doesn't happen in the general population," said Lt. Joseph Badali as he walked through an educational floor of the Twin Towers Correctional Facility during class time. "If you occupy their minds, you don't have violence issues. . . . Everybody can see the positive changes."

Other visitors compared the MERIT barracks to a college dorm where they saw inmates quietly concentrated on studying rather than languishing and napping the hours away. They also noted the amiable, respectful relationships between the inmates and deputies.

More powerful than data and secondhand observations are the

CHAPTER 9

testimonials from MERIT participants themselves and their loved ones. (Their names are withheld for privacy.)

"After entering the education dorm, classes and codes of conduct were initiated to keep peace and provide a place where change from destructive bad behaviors could begin. We forget that a bad attitude, drugs, anger, stealing, not listening to others and not wanting to be a better person all contribute to the cycle of incarceration. It did for me. You changed my life, very profoundly for the better, and I will continue to use and pass on this new information I gained from you and EBI to anyone who will listen to me, especially friends and loved ones."

"I attended The Merit Program at Pitchess Detention Center Jan 24, 2013, for my husband's graduation. . . . I was very pleased with this program and how you are at the front lines giving our inmates another chance at life. I was very touched by your [Lee's] speech to all the inmates, it was almost a father to son talk. I want you to know from the bottom of my heart, 'Thank You Sheriff Baca!' In case you didn't know somebody appreciates the job you do . . . I was amazed at the reaction the inmates displayed toward all the deputies. The energy in the air seemed so strong; it made me forget we were at a jail facility graduation ceremony."

"Ramon was in MCJ MERIT from March December 2012. He learned to type in MERIT. Today, he started a full time job at a prestigious Beverly Hills entertainment law firm, making $50,000/year plus medical and dental. They gave him a test run the last two weeks and he passed. In suit and tie. He would not be employed if it wasn't for the MERIT classes."

"Just wanted to say thank you for everything. It's been very hectic on my side with work and all, but I thought I should give you an update. I have custody of my son. Wow! I can't express to you enough, that I really appreciate all that you have taught me. Not only do I have my son, I've also received a promotion at work and I'm looking into buying a house for my family before spring time. Thank you so much and God Bless."

"Today I am a manager at a large company downtown where I have approximately 120 people I am responsible for. I am of service to AA and members of AA that I can help to change their lives. I have also volunteered with the Five Keys Charter School organization to be part of the group helping others with successful re-entry into society. Lee Baca had a vision which was that education could help reduce recidivism and help successful re-entry into society. I am an example of such a program and there are countless others . . ."

In addition to launching MERIT, Lee approved other programs to minister to the assorted needs of the diverse jail population. It is well known, for example, that gay and transgender inmates endure some of the most violent inmate-on-inmate assaults and rapes in prisons and jails. Under a 1985 consent decree following an ACLU of Southern California lawsuit charging that the department failed to protect

CHAPTER 9

homosexual inmates, Men's Central Jail had established a dedicated housing unit for gay inmates called K6G. Just over ten years later, trans women moved to the protective segregation dorms. By 2012, K6G had an average population of 350 to 400.

When he amended the department's core values to include "courage to stand against racism, sexism, anti-Semitism, homophobia and bigotry in all its forms," Lee walked the walk. He shepherded a plan to recruit more gay and lesbian deputies and to help better protect those in the LGBTQ+ community and repair the department's relationship with them. And whatever monetary curtailments he faced, Lee was set on keeping the K6G dorms intact.

Even the liberal *LA Weekly* had good things to say about the dorm in 2014:

> The gay wing at Men's Central Jail is an exceptionally rare, if not unique, subculture, the only environment of its kind in a major US city. Nothing like it exists in America's 21 largest urban jails, all contacted by the *Weekly*, where officials described in far more modest terms their own steps to deal with and house gay inmates. San Francisco has a transgender housing area, but gay inmates live among the general population. In New York's Rikers Island a similar gay wing was shuttered in 2005.

Before the creation of K6G, many of the LGBTQ+ population were routinely housed in isolation for their own protection and were unable to participate in available educational and vocational programming. Additionally, they required vigilant protection when being escorted through the jail—pulling the limited staff off other duties and putting other inmates at risk under decreased supervision.

By trusting his boots on the ground to create programming in line with the department's core values, thereby eliminating the lengthy approval process up the chain of command, innovation happened faster than usual in the department well known for its bureaucracy. Two years after Lee became sheriff, two K6G deputies, Bart Lanni and Randy Bell, submitted an idea to their captain. With his approval, they launched Social Mentoring Academic and Rehabilitative Training (SMART), which offered K6G inmates daily classes in psychology, yoga and meditation, math, art and music, hypnotherapy as a tool in addiction treatment, as well as other EBI courses.

The majority of the gay and trans population were in jail for drug-related crimes: outright drug offenses and those that support an addict's lifestyle—robbery, burglary, and theft. Without sobriety, the cycle repeats. While recidivism for the general population was usually around 65 percent, in K6G, the lifetime recidivism rate was astronomical at 90 to 95 percent. Yet, after four and a half years, the recidivism rate for SMART graduates had plunged to around 30 percent.

The *LA Weekly* article included a quote from a forty-four-year-old inmate who had spent seventeen years in lockup. "I'm not coming back—I'm done," he said, crediting EBI for his turnaround. "They never had these opportunities that they have now, so EBI is excellent. . . . New Directions is one of [the courses that helped him the most] . . . and Harm Reduction, which teaches you about STIs and HIV testing."

Another inmate said, "The first book I ever read was here." At a SMART graduation ceremony in 2004, a young graduate shared, "I am the most free I've ever been. I am finally able to like me. Today, everything is so bright, even when I close my eyes. I died years ago, and now I'm alive."

GOING OUT: Upon release, inmates return to the same systems that failed to keep them on the straight and narrow. It was impossible for one single institution to completely and permanently undo ingrained

CHAPTER 9

antisocial behavior—not to mention mental illness—where society had failed. It was one thing for inmates to practice their new skills in a sheltered environment with the support of teachers, therapists, and peers, but the outside world wouldn't be as merciful.

According to a 2008 Stanford Law School study, "The seventy-two-hour period immediately following release from prison is a crucial focus for policymakers. This is often a period when parolees need to be connected with housing, counseling, employment, and other resources as smoothly as possible, all this at a time when the parolee is vulnerable to great risks or temptations that may doom chances of successful reentry." Two of the strongest predictors of a return to crime are substance abuse and unemployment.

In 2001 Lee green-lit the launch of the Community Transition Unit (CTU) to connect ex-inmates with public, private, faith-based, and community organizations to promote a seamless, successful reintegration into the community. CTU worked with the EBI Bureau to provide each inmate with a going-out plan, offering reentry assistance with finding employment, tackling substance abuse, and finding government benefits, counseling, and access to medication, housing, and transportation. Though no longer under the purview of the department, keeping inmates from returning to jail was in everyone's best interest. By 2010, forty-three separate public and private organizations had joined the CTU.

A survey found that two years after their release, recidivism amongst participants in one of EBI's drug and alcohol treatment programs was 15 percent below the state average for drug offenders. Similarly, recidivism in one of the domestic violence programs was 21 percent below the county average. And one year after release, the recidivism rate amongst graduates of a program to address homelessness was 28 percent compared to the state average of 41 percent.

By creating EBI, Lee had essentially created a new school district in the county. About EBI's mission, Lee said, "I am trying to trigger self-analysis in all inmates . . . (an) ideological, spiritual conversion from self-doubt and self-loathing to one of possessing strength."

Lee's commitment to assisting released inmates wasn't limited to EBI programming. There was a direct correlation between recidivism, mental illness, and homelessness. Lee had often referred to his jails as "the world's largest mental institution." Forsaken by society and underserved by, or unwilling to seek help from, the public and private agencies designed to support them, the homeless and untreated mentally ill lapped through the jails. Their faces became so familiar, custody personnel referred to them as "frequent flyers." Upon their release, the cycle would start anew. Ill-equipped to better their circumstances, they returned to the only life they knew, one of drugs, alcohol, homelessness, and crime. After slipping through the fingers of family, education, health, and social services systems, the only institution that remained for many was the legal system.

In 2002, about 10 percent of the four hundred prisoners discharged daily from the Twin Towers Correctional Facility had no place to go; estimates put Los Angeles County's homeless population at twenty-five thousand. And in 2020, the Los Angeles Homeless Services Authority reported it had climbed to over sixty-six thousand.

Lee was sorrowed by the whole situation. Frustrated with ineffective existing programs, he felt a moral obligation to use his position and connections to find a solution. A Republican himself, he found an ally in state Senate President Pro Tem John Burton, a San Francisco Democrat, and won a $250,000 grant from the state for research and planning. Working with activists and civic leaders, in the spring of 2002, Lee announced plans for the Homeless Public Safety Center. For $9 million, transitional housing could be built on an abandoned four-acre lot near Twin Towers and Men's Central Jail. The design called for twenty-five green canvas tents, each divided into eight separate pods encircling a shared kitchen, bathroom, and laundry area in a park-like

CHAPTER 9

setting. At $45,000 per pod, the plan was much more cost-effective than other proposed housing solutions.

With security provided by LASD and a program managed by Volunteers of America, the service-resistant would be directed to immediate mental health and medical services, substance abuse treatment, vocational counseling, and assistance in obtaining veterans' and Social Security benefits.

Lee was heralded for his determination and the political risk he was taking by advocating such an audacious idea, but he expectedly faced a landslide of resistance. There were the NIMBYs and those who cited environmental concerns. But a lot of the pushback was from other homeless advocacy groups who jockeyed for every available dollar and thought funding should be earmarked for existing programs. Charles "Bud" Hayes, executive director of the Single Room Occupancy Housing Corporation, told the *Los Angeles Times*, "[Baca] is the only county law enforcement official who's ever taken the time to make an unannounced, non-press-covered walking tour by himself through the toughest parts of skid row and talk to people. He has shown tremendous leadership."

The opposition was too great however, and the Homeless Public Safety Center never came to be. Yet, nearly two decades later, the US Department of Veterans Affairs opened a tent city with a planned capacity of fifty in its Los Angeles parking lot in Westwood and provided medical and psychiatric care, food, bathrooms, showers, and security for veterans without homes. In a pilot program in 2021, the city of Los Angeles set up a similar operation with seventy tents for the public in an East Hollywood parking lot.

Chapter 10

Faith and Heroism

"Faith and heroism are companion tools for success as human beings."

Overlooked and underrepresented ethnic communities had been instrumental in getting Lee elected. And throughout his four terms in office, his attentiveness to their needs never wavered. In the Los Angeles melting pot, residents collectively speak over 185 languages and one of every three people is foreign-born. Many of these immigrants come from countries with unchecked police and political corruption and are naturally distrustful of authority and afraid to report crimes. Part of Lee's Public Trust Policing plan included reaching out to these often disenfranchised factions.

His first success had been in West Hollywood when he was chief of Region II. In addition to repairing the bond with the city's large LGBTQ+ community, he had paid acute attention to the third of the population who came from the South Caucasus area, near Eastern Europe and Western Asia. Deputies introduced themselves to residents to build trust and get a handle on the increasing number of hate crimes directed against these mostly Jewish residents. Lee and department management fostered ties with the Russian Chabad and related ethnic organizations.

One of Lee's first moves after taking office was creating the Asian Crime Task Force. Though Crips, Bloods, and MS-13 gangs dominated the headlines, the county's numerous Asian gangs got little ink or airtime but were just as dangerous and violent, locking the predominantly Asian San Gabriel Valley in fear.

The history of Chinese gangs in Los Angeles can be traced back to the nineteenth century and the California Gold Rush which sparked an influx of three hundred thousand immigrants looking for wealth and work on the Central Pacific Railroad—right when Los Angeles was at the height of its vigilante Wild West heydays. The Chinese opened illegal opium dens and gambling houses in the dusty pueblo's vice district, which was already home to illegal brothels, parlors, and saloons. As rival "tongs"—secret criminally engaged Chinese societies—grew, so did the violence.

On October 23, 1871, a dispute between opposing tongs escalated into a two-day melee, resulting in the shooting of a police officer and murder of the Good Samaritan who had come to his aid. Already harboring a deep, racist contempt for the newcomers, locals were quick to believe a rumor that the Chinese were on a mission to kill anyone white. Hell-bent on revenge, a mob of around five hundred men, women, and children—roughly 10 percent of the community—descended upon the two hundred residents in the burgeoning Chinatown.

Rioters ransacked and robbed Chinese businesses and homes and ruthlessly attacked anyone in their path. Some used pickaxes to create holes in roofs so they could shoot the people inside. Those who ran outside to escape were even easier targets from the shooters' rooftop vantage. The riot became known as the Chinese Massacre of

CHAPTER 10

1871, one of the most significant events in the era's Tong Wars and a foreshadowing of troubled race relations in Los Angeles. Of the seventeen Chinese men and boys killed by the mob, ten of them had been lynched. It was the largest mass lynching in US history, until eleven Italians were lynched in New Orleans twenty years later.

When Lee formed the Asian Task Force, the tongs were all but forgotten, but other Asian gangs had taken root in Los Angeles. Under the influence of foreign syndicates, extortion and robbery were the most common crimes, followed by loansharking, kidnapping, and smuggling. It was well known in law enforcement that—as with other immigrant groups—crimes in the Asian community were underreported. Lee chose bilingual and bicultural deputies to run the new unit and tailor tactical plans to address the complicated situation. Whether from the Philippines, Korea, Indochina, or elsewhere, the gangs' criminal activities were as different as their countries of origin and a one-size-fits-all approach would only end in failure.

Lee's stance against bigotry in all its forms included upholding freedom of religion. He embraced spirituality and faith—regardless of doctrine—understanding them to be essential foundations to building a life of meaning and substance. Though he is Catholic, his children had been raised in the Mormon Church, per his first wife's wishes. Lee's second wife, Carol, is a Buddhist. On weekends he attended services at different churches, synagogues, temples, and mosques. In a 2012 interview with Patt Morrison of the *Los Angeles Times*, Lee explained the relationship he sees between law enforcement and religion: "Society needs to be comforted by the police, not only protected by the police. I think religion offers comfort to people. Religion answers the mystery of life for most people, and faith keeps society moral and doing the right thing for the most part, and law enforcement needs the army of goodness behind it."

The department relied on the support of clergy for their own staff and in the jails. Immediately after being sworn in as sheriff, Lee opened up discussions with religious leaders in L.A. County about the important role they could play in Public Trust Policing. Having earned their congregants' trust, these leaders had far-reaching influence and a unique perspective on their flocks' day-to-day concerns. Lee knew they could play an integral role in improving the LASD's relationship with the public. Rabbis, priests, monks, and imams welcomed Lee's outreach and gave him their support.

When two planes were flown into New York's World Trade Center on September 11, 2001, every American was unwittingly thrust into a new era. While most people were glued to their televisions, trying to process the tragedy, first responders went into action. Lee had just finished his five o'clock morning run and was reading the paper and sipping coffee in his San Marino home when he heard the news.

The LASD began following emergency protocols immediately. When everything was in place, Lee directed his attention to the county's Muslim community. After the attacks, public distrust and suspicion of Muslims and Arabs were instantaneous. If not addressed right away, the situation could have quickly gotten out of hand. Within twenty-four hours, Lee invited sixty religious and ethnic leaders for a confab at LASD headquarters. Having already cultivated close friendships with many of the county's religious leaders, Lee worked with them to quickly establish the Executive Clergy Council, a forum where houses of worship and department leaders could unite to fight and prevent crime and heal the community. Lee later reflected, "I knew we had to get our faith groups working together or hate crimes would evolve to where we have no control."

By September 14, Lee had lists of high-risk targets, including local mosques and Middle Eastern–owned businesses, and he sent deputies to protect them. He wrote to all Los Angeles–area police chiefs, urging them to do the same. Over the next few weeks, Lee spoke at mosques,

CHAPTER 10

the Museum of Tolerance, and the Islamic Center of Northridge. When he spoke at the King Fahd Mosque in Culver City, he asked, "What does God want from us?"

Lee began studying the Quran to better understand Islam. "One of the things I've tried to find out about religion is whether God is ever a criminal accomplice," he said. "And I haven't found that. Not in the Quran, nor in the Bible. There's no evidence that directly links God to criminal acts. Religion should not be portrayed as an accomplice of murder. Those who use it that way are casting a dark cloud on their faith."

While Lee pondered macro issues, he didn't forget the micro. He met with Muslim shop owners and encouraged them to report hate crimes. When he heard from one of his deputies that his young son was afraid and embarrassed to wear his turban, Lee invited both to his office so he could listen to the boy's concerns and provide gentle counsel. Thereafter, he heard, the boy wore his turban proudly and wanted to join the department once he was old enough.

Though formed in response to the 2001 backlash against Muslims, the Executive Clergy Council took hold and still plays an important role in Los Angeles today. It grew from fifty men and women from various Eastern and Western religions to include thousands. Council members met regularly to sustain their relationships with each other and the sheriff's department and to tackle complex community issues. A representative from each of the twenty-three sheriff's stations volunteered to serve on the council. By having a personal relationship with faith-based leaders, Lee and his deputies could enlist their help in diffusing potentially volatile situations before they became a problem. In turn, the clergy could offer perspective on any of their faiths' customs and beliefs that might affect their interaction with deputies. The insight would be used in training to diffuse tension within and between the department and the public. The clergy had their fingers on the pulse of the communities they served, as well as direct experience with hate crimes. The relationships formed among the groups themselves and with the department were mutually beneficial. Lee faithfully attended their monthly meetings.

Unequivocally, one of Lee's greatest talents is bringing people together for the common good. In 2011, he urged the council to offer drug education for local clergy by partnering with the Los Angeles–based nonprofit Foundation for a Drug-Free World. After two weeks of training, over one hundred clergy were certified as Drug-Free World Prevention Specialists, empowered with new skills to help their congregants.

The Executive Clergy Council hosted outreach events such as Community Day and Unity Day—opportunities for members of diverse congregations to unite with sheriff's deputies over food, live music, and games. Community Day included a job fair and clothing and school backpack giveaways.

The council's Multi-Faith Prayer Breakfast, which attracted 2,000 attendees to its sixth event, was recognized as one of the largest interfaith prayer breakfasts in the nation. For comparison, the National Prayer Breakfast in Washington, DC, has an annual attendance of around 3,500. Secular agencies including the FBI, the Drug Enforcement Administration, the LAPD, and community organizations such as Stop the Violence Increase the Peace Foundation supported the breakfast.

The Executive Clergy Council was actively present in the jails. Members underwent comprehensive training to teach EBI life skills classes. Appreciating how many lives are affected by a loved one's incarceration, Lee encouraged the council to partner with Prison Fellowship Angel Tree, a nonprofit that ministers to the nation's prison population and their families. A 2000 report by the California Research Bureau estimated "approximately 195,000 children currently have parents in state prison, 97,000 have parents in jail, and 564,000 children

CHAPTER 10

have parents on parole or probation." Through Angel Tree toy drives, inmates in L.A. County jails who had little contact with their children were able to give them gifts over the holidays.

Lee's support for the Muslim community extended beyond the Executive Clergy Council and continued long after the 9/11 attacks. Following federal agencies' counterterrorism efforts which focused on surveillance, profiling, deportations, and "If you see something, say something," Muslim and Arab communities felt targeted and assumed to be guilty by association. Knowing a hostile approach would only deepen the schisms between "us" and "them" Lee worked to repair the relationship. As he explained, it came down to trust. "It's extremely effective to have positive interactions with the community . . . And what we've seen is that the Muslim community is as eager to help as anyone. It's not about spying on the community but about building public trust."

When radicalized British citizens killed fifty-two people in the 2005 London subway bombings, Lee realized he needed to do more to thwart homegrown terrorism. If the Muslim community came to truly trust the department, he knew they would be more willing to offer tips on suspected plots. He instructed deputies to be exceedingly responsive to even the most minor calls and created the Muslim-American Homeland Security Congress. The organization was a first-of-its-kind nonprofit with no political, governmental, or religious ties. It would build a bridge between the LASD and the Muslim community, supporting imams in speaking out against terrorism and identifying people with extremist leanings to strengthen local and national security.

Lee demonstrated his support of Islamic Angelenos by quoting passages from the Quran, kneeling and pressing his head to the floor in prayer at mosques, learning some Farsi and Urdu, and dancing with abandon in cultural celebrations. His fealty didn't dim with time. Over the following years, he created the Muslim Community Outreach Program and the Muslim American Leaders Advisory Council (YoungMALAC). In keeping with his commitment to public-trust policing, Lee launched the department's Muslim Community Affairs Unit (MCA) in 2008. Staffed by Arabic-speaking Muslim deputies, the unit strengthened the relationship between the Muslim community and the department for the benefit of both. MCA provided educational programs on domestic violence response, gang activity awareness, driver's education, and identity theft avoidance. Creating meaningful relationships led to increased trust, which opened doors for early tips about potential dangers. With time, the deputies were able to encourage cooperation with other law enforcement agencies, including the LAPD, FBI, US Department of Homeland Security, and more.

The concern and care Lee showed the Muslim community placed him on the national and world stage. He had become a voice for the oft-maligned group and was a sought-after speaker on counterterrorism. On March 17, 2010, he testified before the House of Representatives Committee on Homeland Security Subcommittee on Intelligence, Information Sharing, and Terrorism Risk Assessment for the second time, for the hearing on "Working with Communities to Disrupt Terror Plots." In a sharp navy suit and striped tie with a matching pocket handkerchief, Lee stressed the importance of local police building trust and authentic relationships with their Muslim communities. "Information that is relationship-derived is more reliable than information twice or more removed from the original source," he said.

Promoting local policing as a first line of defense in the US's fight against terrorism, Lee offered a four-step approach that included public-trust policing, calling on Muslim communities to actively participate in preventative measures, professional international police diplomacy, and interfaith respect.

Over the years, Lee had weathered grillings from the L.A. County

CHAPTER 10

Board of Supervisors with grace and aplomb, rarely displaying the frustration and anger he surely must have felt. But when Representative Mark Souder, a Republican from Indiana, implied that Lee supported the fundamentalist militant organization Hamas by attending fundraisers for the Council on American Islamic Relations (CAIR), Lee's response was swift and passionate. In a heated exchange with Souder, Lee avowed his fervent support for Israel: "Where were you when Israel needed an ally in local law enforcement? I was there. The security of Israel has always been at the forefront of my thinking. For you to associate me somehow through some circuitous attack on CAIR is not only inappropriate, it is un-American."

The following year, per Mississippi Democrat congressman Bennie Thompson's request, Lee was invited back to testify on the hearing for "The Extent of Radicalization in the American Muslim Community and that Community's Response." The committee's chairman Peter King, a Republican from New York, had called the controversial hearing. Critics—Muslim and not—were incensed that singling out Muslims and not addressing white supremacists and gangs with ties to cartels would only fuel Islamophobia. Privacy, civil rights, and civil liberties were all under attack.

In his opening statement, Lee made his position clear:

> I would caution that to comment only on the extent of radicalization in the Muslim American community may be viewed as singling out a particular section of our nation. This makes a false assumption that any particular religion or group is more prone to radicalization than others. For example, according to information provided by the Congressional Research Service, there have been seventy-seven total terror plots by domestic non-Muslim perpetrators since 9/11. In comparison, there have been forty-one total plots by both domestic

and international Muslim perpetrators during the same period.

Reports indicate that Muslim Americans helped foil seven of the last ten plots propagated by al-Qaeda within the United States. Evidence clearly indicates a general rise of violent extremism across ideologies. Therefore, we should be examining radicalization as an issue that affects all groups, regardless of religion. It is counterproductive to build trust when individuals or groups claim that Islam supports terrorism. This plays directly into the terrorist propaganda that the West's war on terror is actually a war against Islam. It is critical to build mutually respectful relationships with Muslim American communities in an endeavor to work together to protect all Americans.

Lee's engagement with Muslim Americans made him an easy target for critics, who questioned his patriotism and worried he was taking a soft stance on terrorism. The $750,000 he raised for New York police and firefighters didn't make the news; nor did all the threats to the city and county that his network had thwarted.

Chapter 11

Cooperation and Global Diplomacy

"All cultures are desirous of peaceful relations. Law enforcement must play a vital role in achieving such harmony."

During a 1980 business lunch, an NYPD official and an FBI special agent brainstormed how they could work together to determine who was responsible for a recent slew of violent attacks in the city. Their brainstorming led to the creation of the FBI's Joint Terrorism Task Force (JTTF) division. JTTFs are multi-agency investigative units that create channels between the FBI and local, state, and federal agencies to share intelligence and resources. Setting aside jurisdictional boundaries, the FBI's National Joint Terrorism Task Force cut some of the bureaucratic red tape that restricted local agencies' access to crucial classified information. Today, there are nearly two hundred JTTFs working from FBI field offices, but before the World Trade attacks there were only twenty-six. In 1986, the LASD and LAPD united to join the National Joint Terrorism Task Force. As a JTTF, Los Angeles sheriff's and police departments had access to FBI specialists, including analysts, linguists, and investigators. In turn, the FBI gained a network of boots on the ground and a rapport with city and county SWAT teams.

Five years before 9/11, LASD's Sergeant John P. Sullivan and Deputy Larry Richards shared their mutual concern over a fatwa entitled "Declaration of War against the Americans Occupying the Land of the Two Holy Places" issued by a virtually unknown member of the mujahideen Afghan resistance movement: Osama Bin Laden. In studying the increasing danger of terrorism on US soil, Sullivan and Richards saw heinous acts were plotted through a widespread sophisticated and expanding web. Attacks on major US cities could originate overseas and be executed by cells of seemingly unrelated conspirators hiding in plain sight in any small American town. If terrorists operated successfully through such a complex network, Sullivan and Richards thought a similar system might facilitate counterterrorism efforts.

This was the beginning of the county's Terrorist Early Warning (TEW) group, which went beyond JTTF efforts to track emerging terrorist threats and prevent them by expanding their partnership to include other first responders—including local branches of the military; hospital networks and the county's Department of Public Health; area fire and police departments, and more—to come up with preparedness and response plans for L.A. County. TEW sought to address intelligence gaps and upend the practice of withholding information rather than sharing it across agencies.

TEW operated under the LASD Emergency Operations Bureau. Terrorism liaison officers appointed from each represented agency created "playbooks" outlining plans of action in the event of cyberterrorism and chemical, biological, and nuclear agents. TEW also created Response Information Folders—detailed action plans for an inventory of high-risk targets such as airports, tourist attractions, movie studios, power plants, and mass transit—and oversaw training

CHAPTER 11

exercises for potential attacks on specific locations. TEW responded to 1998's anthrax hoax and organized preparations for Y2K and the 2000 Democratic National Convention. The US Department of Homeland Security recognized TEW as "a best practice for replication throughout the country." For his work on TEW, Lee is recognized in *Terrorism Early Warning: 10 Years of Achievement in Fighting Terrorism and Crime*: "[TEW] has benefited from the continuing support of Sheriff Lee Baca, who has demonstrated that he is not averse to unorthodox views and unconventional approaches to law enforcement."

Because the LASD already had action plans in place through the JTTF and TEW, along with the department's own Counter-Terrorism Unit, Lee had received immediate assessments on—and secured—all of the recognized hard targets in Los Angeles County within two hours of the attacks on the Twin Towers.

Once certain Los Angeles was safe, Lee had collaborated with California Governor Gray Davis and Attorney General Dan Lungren to create the California Anti-Terrorism Information Center. Within two weeks of the World Trade Center attacks, a *Los Angeles Times* article reported Lee as the chair of a fourteen-member advisory board that would form what was essentially a statewide version of the county's TEW. Punctuating the importance of police and sheriff's departments in combating global and homegrown terrorism, Lee stated, "When we look back at past tragedies such as the Oklahoma City bombing . . . it was a patrol officer on a [country] road that captured Timothy McVeigh."

With an executive order, Davis launched the Governor's Office of Homeland Security in 2003. Lee was appointed Director of Homeland Security, Mutual Aid for California Region 1, putting the safety of Los Angeles and Orange counties' thirteen million residents in his hands. In the event of an emergency, he would receive mutual aid requests and coordinate assistance from governmental agencies as well as those such as the American Red Cross and the Salvation Army. In this role, Lee documented terrorist threats and commanded multiple dire situations, including the Chatsworth train collision, in which twenty-five souls were lost.

One of the difficulties first responders faced in New York on 9/11 was that their radios couldn't communicate with each other. Tragically, calls between the NYPD and NYFD disappeared into the ether. In Los Angeles County at that time, emergency services used over forty different radio systems (many of which were outdated). A uniform network was critical to keep the public safe in times of disaster and terror, so Lee worked with other county agencies, fire chiefs, and police chiefs to create the Los Angeles Regional Interoperable Communications System. He raised $300 million from the Department of Homeland Security and $150 million from the Department of Transportation to develop a unified regional voice and data system for public safety responders.

In their joint efforts to protect the city and county, Lee and LAPD Chief William Bratton formed a powerful and united front. After profiling the chief in the Aspen Institute report "Los Angeles' Preparedness for Terrorism," former Inspector General of the United States Department of Homeland Security Clark Kent Ervin wrote, "In his efforts to combat terrorism in the Los Angeles area, Bratton is complemented by an equally insightful, imaginative, and aggressive sheriff in Lee Baca. The two work so closely that Bratton joked that they spend more time with each other than their respective wives."

The sheriff and the chief joined the FBI, California and US Departments of Homeland Security, and US Attorney to open the Joint Regional Intelligence Center (JRIC) in 2006. Sixty analysts from the JTTF, LASD, and LAPD relocated to the seventh floor of a county office building in Norwalk to run the state-of-art command center. Serving as a 24/7 hub to manage integrated counterterrorism intelligence for Los Angeles and surrounding counties, the JRIC was the

CHAPTER 11

first regional "fusion center" in the DHS's national network. Using Los Angeles's JRIC as a model, then-governor Arnold Schwarzenegger authorized funding for three additional centers for the rest of the state.

For Lee, commanding the largest sheriff's department in the world came with a moral obligation to act whenever he could use his position to effect positive change. Having traveled throughout the world and confabbed with law enforcement officials in cultures operating under a broad spectrum of philosophies and civil liberties, Lee had a unique and profound understanding of the art of policing. His inbox filled with invitations from Congress, media outlets, universities, and even foreign governments keen for his input and insight into law enforcement and counterterrorism,

His search for a deeper understanding of Middle Eastern issues and cultures to build bridges and fight terrorism had led Lee to the Levant several times. "I knew that if I was going to serve the public safety needs of a diverse people, I was going to need to understand people [from there] more thoroughly," he said.

When former Secretary of State Warren Christopher introduced Lee to Pakistan's President Pervez Musharraf, who was visiting California in 2003, Lee expressed interest in learning anti-terrorism strategies from a country with firsthand experience with the terrorist group Al Qaeda. Musharraf extended an invitation, and despite warnings from the US State Department, Lee; his wife, Carol; a couple LASD deputies; members of the Southeast Asian Advisory Committee; and three sheriffs from Sacramento, Alabama, and New Jersey journeyed to Pakistan in February 2004. Lee paid for Carol's ticket; his was subsidized by private donors.

When the delegation visited a military outpost overlooking the Afghan border, after driving past signs warning "Foreigners Prohibited," Ted Sexton, the sheriff from Alabama, spoke up: "I've done some stupid things with you, Lee, but this has got to be the stupidest." With their nine-day itinerary documented by local media, the group was an easy target for Al Qaeda. Undeterred, Lee was able to set up an exchange program with the Islamabad Police Department and attended a summit with Pakistani intelligence agencies. They briefed him on counterterrorism operations and an investigation into a recent assassination attempt on Musharraf.

Later, Lee attended an outdoor barbecue in his honor. To the amusement of the other guests, Lee took Carol's hand and danced Zorba-style to a military band playing a Pakistani song. Of the only couple dancing, one guest was quoted saying, "It's very nice to see a police official dancing. Most of the times they are making other people dance."

Invitations poured in from Armenia, Azerbaijan, the Emirates, Egypt, Jordan, Lebanon, Qatar, Russia, Saudi Arabia, and Turkey for Lee to lecture on policing, collaborate on theoretical and operative solutions to terrorism, and build diplomatic relationships. Over his years with the LASD, Lee made multiple trips to Israel. Enforcing the law in the only democracy in the Middle East, Israeli police were held to a standard that mirrored America's when it came to upholding citizens' constitutional rights and answering to the public and a free press. And having fought terrorism for decades, the Israel National Police held the distinction of operating law enforcement's most sophisticated systems of intelligence, deterrence, response, and trauma.

Lee participated in many of the Israel National Police's seminars and conferences on global terror. Topics included intelligence gathering, tactical medical training, de-escalation techniques, and more. Attendees toured the country's Emergency Management Agency, security training facilities, police headquarters, and trauma centers.

Concerned Hamas was building tunnels under the Gaza-Israel border, Israel Defense Forces broke an established ceasefire and launched an onslaught of airstrikes against Hamas targets in Gaza on December 27, 2008. Hamas retaliated, launching unguided missiles

CHAPTER 11

into Israel. Twelve days later, Lee was on a plane to Tel Aviv. County supervisor Zev Yaroslavsky wanted the county's top crime fighter to witness firsthand how Israeli first responders managed the crisis. When Hamas launched a Qassam rocket attack against Sderot, an Israeli city Lee was visiting less than a mile from Gaza, he got a closer firsthand look than he and Yaroslavsky had anticipated. Lee was unharmed but over a thousand lost their lives in the three-week conflict.

In our modern era, no country's borders are impenetrable. Tunnels can be dug, walls can be climbed, and technology can be hacked. Cyberterrorists don't need passports and visas to wreak havoc on our infrastructure and national security. While the media warns of Russian and Chinese hackers, an acne-riddled thirteen-year-old ensconced in his parents' basement is just as dangerous. The days of a beat cop worrying about only his assigned neighborhood are as much a thing of the past as white tennis balls and New Coke.

Lee's office bookshelf held a collection of law enforcement officers' hats from around the world. In his travels he had developed exchange programs for his department to train with other international agencies and vice versa. The LASD training facility was world-renowned, and the Special Enforcement Bureau had hosted members of police and special force units from South America, Europe, and the Middle East.

Protecting a county perched on the Pacific Rim, a two-hour drive from Mexico, and home to the busiest port in the Western Hemisphere, Lee had vast experience with international crime. He had worked intimately with the FBI and other countries on matters involving drug cartels, gangs, smuggling exotic species, human trafficking, and federal extraditions. He had relationships with kings and presidents. He knew more leaders in military and police on six continents than he could count. Together, they were a global police community—and Lee recognized the powerful difference such a network could make in fighting modern crime.

SHERIFF LEE BACA

In 2009, the LASD published Lee's ideas in *Police Diplomacy: A Global Trust*, which promoted "the interchange of policing resources, training, and experience between nations to enhance public participation and provide a safer, more secure community regardless of geopolitical borders." The next step in Public Trust Policing, it applied the same principles on a much larger scale. The booklet provided examples of how to develop global participation through cultural exchange programs, donating replaced safety equipment to underequipped agencies, and proactively finding opportunities to share ideas with other countries' defense units.

When Lee testified before the House Committee on Homeland Security Subcommittee on Intelligence, Information Sharing, and Terrorism Risk Assessment in 2008, he expressed his frustrations that operational intelligence withheld from local agencies was impeding counterterrorism efforts, the JRIC wasn't getting enough federal funding, and America's nineteen thousand police and sheriff's departments didn't function as a national police system when dealing with foreign countries.

He concluded his testimony by adding:

> There has to be an international police diplomacy program. I have been to so many countries in the Middle East, and in my testimony you will see all of them. I have spoken to President Musharraf, I have spoken to King Abdullah, I have spoken to the intelligence director of Saudi Arabia, including Qatar. These individuals are not reluctant to tell us the kind of information we need to know so that we in the United States can have a greater sensitivity as to how the terrorists are operating in countries that I have mentioned.
>
> So, clearly, what I am saying is that there is a need

CHAPTER 11

to expand our international reach through perhaps a committee or a group of major-city chiefs and sheriffs, and minor-city chiefs and sheriffs for that matter, who would do what has to be done to create the inter-communicative skills that we need with our counterparts internationally.

Chapter 12

The Sting and the Judge

*"The 10 percent of those who don't represent our
Core Values are hurting all the rest who do."*

When a twelve-minute slow-speed chase through Compton came to an end just after midnight on May 9, 2005, ten LASD deputies fired 120 rounds of ammunition at the vehicle's driver with no plan or consideration of the risk to their fellow officers, let alone neighbors in the area. Miraculously, no one was killed, but the suspect and one deputy were hit.

The following day, accompanied by the Reverend Al Sharpton, Lee went door to door to listen to residents' fear and anger as they showed him the bullet holes in their homes. He apologized and denounced the shootings. That night at a town hall meeting, he offered compensation for property damages and accepted the onslaught of criticism, saying, "We're not here to twist it, we're not here to sugarcoat anything, we're here to tell it exactly like it is—the good, the bad, and the ugly." Days after the shooting, nine of the ten deputies involved offered an unprecedented public apology.

Out of the public's eye, Lee acted swiftly, immediately ordering an Internal Affairs investigation, as well as discipline of the deputies. His department studied and revised policy and training practices to ensure such an incident would never happen again. The OIR's subsequent investigation found the deputies had ignored orders to disperse at the end of the pursuit and set up a perimeter. OIR concurred with the LASD's own findings that "the performance of nearly all the officers and one of the supervisors was substandard and, in some cases, substantially below standard."

The year 2005 also marked the installation of seventy-five closed-circuit cameras at Pitchess, the start of construction on the Herzberg-Davis Crime Lab, and the destruction of six tons of illegal weapons confiscated by county officers. It's possible one of the destroyed guns belonged to Anthony Brown, who was in state prison after being convicted for three bank robberies that year. Upon his July 2009 parole, Brown immediately kicked off a cocaine-fueled crime spree through Los Angeles, after which he was accused of robbing a Rite Aid, El Pollo Loco, Denny's, and several banks. During one of the robberies, he carried a toy gun, but later got a real gun and fired it at a victim, earning him an attempted murder charge. Dubbed the "Do-Rag Bandit," Brown had but one month on the outside before he was sent to Men's Central Jail with no bail.

On June 27, 2011, Brown was found guilty on ten counts of armed robbery, one count of attempted murder, and one weapons violation. He was sentenced to 423 years to life. It was while he was at Men's Central Jail awaiting transfer to state prison that the FBI recruited Brown as an informant in their investigation into deputy abuses in the Los Angeles jails.

Los Angeles County jails had been under scrutiny for decades by

CHAPTER 12

the FBI, the ACLU, the media, and the public—and also by the OIR and PARC. Whereas his predecessors had discouraged and thwarted external investigations, Lee had laid a welcome mat and received any findings that showed failures and deficiencies in operation.

Back when Lee was a lieutenant working at Carson Station in 1975, the ACLU had filed a lawsuit on behalf of all detainees in the Men's Central Jail. *Rutherford v. Pitchess* alleged inmates' constitutional rights were being violated, citing overcrowded conditions, poor medical care, and abuse of prisoners by deputies. In his decision, District Judge William P. Gray ruled in favor of the detainees, citing overcrowded and inadequate cell space. Built in 1963, MCJ's cells are four by eight feet, affording each inmate thirty-two square feet of living space. At the time of Judge Gray's 1978 ruling, correctional standards required fifty square feet. (Today, the American Correctional Association's standards are seventy feet.)

The judge also affirmed concerns about insufficient recreation, unclean clothing, and lengthy processing times. Concurrently, he expressed his understanding of the county's budgetary problems in the face of Proposition 13. In the judgment that followed, he ordered the sheriff's department to make twelve different changes in jail conditions. Negotiations and appeals between the court and the department were still ongoing when Sherman Block became sheriff in 1982. The case went all the way to the US District Court for the Central District of California, the Ninth Circuit Court of Appeals, and the US Supreme Court. *Rutherford v. Pitchess* became *Rutherford v. Block*, which then became *Rutherford v. Baca*.

Whatever the legal wrangling, one thing was clear: The Los Angeles County jail system was overwhelmed. Its services were hindered by physical constraints, overcrowding from external pressures, and chronic underfunding. When the ACLU threatened to sue the county again in 1985, the two bodies agreed to a compromise in which the ACLU became a court-appointed monitor of the jails.

SHERIFF LEE BACA

In 1994, California voters approved Proposition 184, the Three Strikes Sentencing Initiative, mandating that anyone with two prior violent or serious felony convictions who committed a third felony of *any* type received a life sentence, with a minimum imprisonment of twenty-five years.

The California Ballot Pamphlet for the November general election erroneously summarized that there would be "no direct fiscal impact resulting from this measure." But the effect on the state's county criminal justice systems was immediate. An estimated 90 to 97 percent of state sentencing is determined through the plea bargain process. But with any felony considered a third strike, someone found guilty of buying a stolen vehicle, impersonating someone else, or using gill nets to catch salmon, steelhead, or striped bass could end up in prison for life. Cases that previously would have been settled in a plea bargain were now heard in lengthy jury trials while the defendants remained in county jails. Given the possible outcome of a life sentence, bail was doubled or not even an option for third-strikers, who were also considered high-risk inmates and needed to be housed away from the general population. In already overcrowded jails, sheriffs and police across the state had no option other than issuing early releases to lower-level offenders, despite the public's swift outrage. Los Angeles County jails were stretched to their limit, as was the frustration tolerance of inmates and deputies alike.

In 1996, two years after the three-strikes law went into effect, the Department of Justice informed then-Sheriff Block it would be investigating allegations of civil rights violations against the incarcerated mentally ill under the Civil Rights of the Institutionalized Persons Act. The US DOJ listed numerous problems with the county's treatment of these inmates, as well as inadequate mental health care and excessive use of force by deputies. In March 2008, the ACLU asked Dr. Terry Kupers, an expert on correctional mental health issues, to investigate L.A. County jails. After weeks of observation, reviewing

CHAPTER 12

documents, and interviewing inmates, deputies, and medical personnel, Dr. Kupers made multiple recommendations. The first was to: "Significantly decrease the population of Los Angeles County Jail." Dr. Kupers urged for increased programming to address boredom, reducing harsh lighting and noise levels, separating the mentally ill from the general population, minimizing isolation, and expanding mental health services. The bottom line was that the jails needed to increase services and staff.

Just when it felt like the situation couldn't get any worse, in 2011, Governor Jerry Brown signed Assembly Bill 109 in reaction to a Supreme Court order requiring California to reduce its state prison population to no more than 137.5 percent of its design capacity within two years. At the time, California prisons were operating at 180 percent capacity. And as so often happens in politics, the state passed the buck. State prisoners were reassigned to the equally overcrowded county jails.

But that wasn't all. In 2011, the titanic Los Angeles County jail system finally collided with the glacial mass it had been heading towards for years. and the collateral damage was concussive.

Bad things happen in jails, and Men's Central Jail was no exception. In fact, it had long been considered one of the worst in the country. On top of the aforementioned failures, there were reports of deputy cliques and gut-wrenching stories of deputy-on-inmate violence. Investigations into deputy force issues were notoriously difficult and protracted. Inmates and officers alike were naturally biased toward their peers and made difficult witnesses. Cameras helped, but there weren't enough to cover every square foot of jail.

While Lee was looking to reform the jails through EBI, he relied on his trusted second-in-command, Undersheriff Paul Tanaka, to oversee force investigations and discipline. The undersheriff also managed the department's finances and many of its day-to-day operations. Lee respected Tanaka's can-do attitude and was mentoring him to take the reins when he retired. The two made an interesting pair. In her 2015 *Los Angeles Magazine* piece, Celeste Fremon wrote, "Tanaka, who is fifty-five, provided the perfect counterpoint to Baca's guru persona. For instance, Tanaka thrived on confrontation. . . . If Baca was the empathy-driven futurist, the philosopher king, Tanaka was a detail guy who could drive a project from start to finish, micromanaging obsessively when he thought a matter important."

After multiple well-documented cases of deputies using inexplicable and brutal force—one of which the ACLU monitor actually witnessed in 2009—the FBI launched another investigation into the jails in 2011. That same year, in its scathing report "Cruel and Usual Punishment: How a Savage Gang of Deputies Controls L.A. County Jails," the ACLU called for Lee's resignation.

After hearing about the 2009 ACLU-witnessed jail incident Lee was informed of another. That same year, a chaplain in the jails had seen a group of deputies beating an inmate on the 3000 bloc of Men's Central Jail. Shaken, the chaplain submitted a detailed report of the event to the LASD. When he followed up with Lee two years later, the sheriff was caught completely by surprise. Witnesses reported that he looked at his executive staff and cried, "This happened two years ago and I'm only finding out about it now?" He reviewed the case file. The chaplain's report was nowhere to be found, but there was a note that his account had exaggerated the details of the beating.

The Board of Supervisors, the US Attorney, the media, and the public also clamored for accountability and justice. Lee didn't have all the answers they were looking for, but he wouldn't rest until he unearthed the breakdown. He launched a series of individual deep-dive meetings with top command and explained to the *Los Angeles Times*, "Everyone wants to handle it; they believe it's their job but handling it and not telling me leaves me vulnerable. . . . I have to be informed." He admitted, "I wasn't ignoring the jails. I just didn't know. People

CHAPTER 12

can say, 'What the hell kind of leader is that?' The truth is I should've known."

On September 25, 2011, the Sunday edition of the *Times* bore the headline, "FBI probes jail beating allegations: Agents sneaked a phone to an informant without telling Baca." The informant was Anthony Brown, the "Do-Rag Bandit" serving 423 years for armed robbery. And though most inmate informants are engaged to snitch on other inmates, Brown had been solicited to provide evidence of deputy corruption and abuse. Under the FBI's direction, in 2009, Brown bribed a custody deputy to smuggle him a cell phone. The deputy had no idea Brown's "friend" on the outside who covertly handed him the phone and cash was an undercover FBI agent. Notably, in its years of service, the FBI had never inserted contraband of any type into a jail before. Brown had the phone for three weeks before deputies at Men's Central Jail found it in a Doritos bag during a random cell search. The phone had photographs of cocaine, heroin, methamphetamines, and ecstasy, but no pictures of deputies' engaged in excessive force. Sheriff's deputies purportedly later threatened the lead FBI agent at her home.

The chain of events that followed triggered a Federal Grand Jury investigation, which ultimately led to the indictment of over eighteen LASD officials. Not a target of the investigation himself, Lee was publicly blamed for the debacle, as well as every other problem in the LASD. He took it in stride, focusing on the work ahead. He fast-tracked jail reforms that had been under review, investigated disciplinary procedures, instituted more frequent personnel rotations, and found solutions to reduce the amount of time academy graduates spent working in custody. He was sickened by the stories of misconduct he was only now learning about, and without diminishing the excessive violence, he reminded himself the eighteen indicted deputies made up just .01 percent of the eighteen thousand employees he managed.

In June 2013, Lee was named Sheriff of the Year by his peers at the

National Sheriff's Association annual conference in Charlotte, North Carolina. That year, Los Angeles County had its lowest number of homicides since 1970.

Spurred by the allegations of abuse, the Board of Supervisors appointed a Citizens' Commission on Jail Violence. Its 2012 report listed their findings and recommended reforms pertaining to use of force, management, culture, personnel, discipline, and oversight. Though critical of department leadership, the report acknowledged:

> [The Sheriff's] senior leaders failed to monitor conditions in the jails and elevate use of force issues so that they received the necessary attention by the Sheriff, and the Undersheriff engaged in conduct that undermined supervision of aggressive deputies and promoted an environment of lax and untimely discipline of deputy misconduct. With multiple command layers between the jails and the Sheriff, there was no one in the Department who was responsible *and* accountable to the Sheriff for addressing the force problems in the jails. . . . Department leaders have undermined the investigative and discipline systems by inappropriate comments and conduct and the Commission has seen evidence suggesting that acts of dishonesty are not always subject to the "zero tolerance" philosophy articulated by the Sheriff.

For years, Lee had considered Paul Tanaka his heir apparent, but the undersheriff had become a prominent—and much maligned—player in the investigations into the Los Angeles County jails. Under protest, Tanaka resigned in March 2013, but in the summer he announced he would run against his mentor in the 2014 sheriff's election. Tanaka

CHAPTER 12

came out swinging. In a chilling reminder of when he had run against Sherman Block, Lee feared the contest would divide the department once again. Hard-nosed old-schoolers liked Tanaka's take-no-prisoners attitude, while the more progressive remained loyal to Lee's public-trust policing. And as he had when running against Block, Lee vowed to run a clean campaign.

During this time, Carol was visiting her father in Taiwan when she got an urgent email from one of Lee's secretaries asking her to return to the US immediately. He was worried about Lee's health. Lee hadn't wanted to alarm Carol, but when she got home, he explained that one day his brain had "shut down" for an hour, during which he couldn't remember a thing. He was unnerved, as was Carol. They attributed it—as well as his uncharacteristic forgetfulness of late—to the enormous stress he was under. They wondered if it was time for him to retire and fantasized about the traveling they would be able to do. But first, Lee needed to see his doctor.

Soon after the lapse, one of the assistant sheriffs informed Lee that the campaign was indeed having an adverse effect on the spirit in the department and deputies felt like it was impacting their ability to do their work. Lee took the weekend to contemplate his part in creating the general malaise. Intuitive and decisive, Lee had often caught his family and closest confidantes by surprise. By Monday he had made a decision. He met with his top brass, one by one, and notified the Board of Supervisors that he would retire in three weeks. At a January 7, 2014, press conference in front of the Monterey Park headquarters, Lee, choking back emotion, made the following statement:

> I want to make a few thank-yous. First of all, thank you all for being here. We've had a great journey over the years, speaking to one another about important issues facing the county of Los Angeles regarding

crime, our successes, and the things we've tried to do. But I also want to thank a couple of people who certainly were instrumental in my life. First of all, Sheriff Peter J. Pitchess, who promoted me to captain, and Sherman Block, who promoted me to division chief. Both of my predecessors were my mentors and my teachers. As I always like to say, "If you want to know who I am, I'm my teachers." And I've learned a lot. And I've been proud and honored to serve the Los Angeles County Sheriff's Department and the people of this greatest of counties, Los Angeles County, for the past forty-eight years. I can't even imagine anyone working forty-eight years at anything. But I've done that, which has made this decision in my life probably the most difficult.

The duties of a sheriff are too complex and too vast to describe simply, but all the people in this county count. Everybody. And the men and women of the sheriff's department and I are dedicated to the welfare of the people of this county. It doesn't matter who they are, what their difficulties may be. They're always at the foremost of our thoughts and mind. So, therefore, I have great gratitude for the people who have elected me. And at the same time, that I was elected to four terms, I will go out on my terms. I'm not going to seek reelection for a fifth term as sheriff and I will retire at the end of this month.

The reasons for doing so are so many. Some are most personal and private. But the prevailing one is the negative

CHAPTER 12

perception this upcoming campaign has brought to the exemplary service provided by the men and women of the sheriff's department. They have conducted themselves with the utmost integrity and professionalism, resulting in yet another year of historic crime reductions in nearly half a century. In my opinion, your sheriff's department is the greatest law enforcement agency in the world. I want to thank the men and women of the Los Angeles County Sheriff's Department for their hard work, dedication, and their daily sacrifices to serve the great people of this county.

It wouldn't be an exaggeration to say that we love the people of this county. And we do it every day, without exception. And to the people of the county, I extend my deepest gratitude for you allowing me to serve you for the past forty-eight years. It has been a true dream come true to meet so many incredible people of all races, all religions, all nationalities, and all statuses. I especially care about the homeless, the mentally ill, and the people that are in challenges much greater than I've ever faced. And so, in conclusion, as your elected sheriff for the past fifteen years, I've held fast to the Core Values of this great department. And they are, of which every deputy remembers by heart, as I do, as follows:

As a leader in the Los Angeles County Sheriff's Department, I will commit myself to honorably perform my duties with respect for the dignity of all people, the integrity to do right and fight what is wrong, wisdom

> to apply common sense and fairness in all that I do, and the courage to stand against racism, sexism, anti-Semitism, homophobia, and bigotry in all its forms.
>
> That's who I am. That's who we are. It's our great nation and our great nation's laws that we love and respect.

In the Q and A that followed, Lee added, "I didn't want to enter a campaign that would be full of contentious negative politicking. I wanted to realize within myself that there has to be another future for the sheriff's department. And I was confident that people inside the sheriff's department are capable of doing this work." He went on, "I may have run seventy thousand miles in my lifetime, but I know I'm seventy-two years old in May and I don't see myself as the future. I see myself as part of the past. What's more important is to give others inside the sheriff's department a chance who I know would not take the chance if I were to run again. . . . The answer is the nobility of having served and knowing when it's time to let someone else."

Six months after Lee's announcement, six of the eighteen LASD deputies who had been indicted, were found guilty of conspiracy and obstruction of justice. Evidence revealed that after Anthony Brown had been discovered, deputies had covertly transferred him to different jails using pseudonyms and missing fingerprint records to hide him from his FBI handlers—all while the FBI and the US Marshals had been trying to transfer Brown to state prison. The accused deputies claimed they were following orders from above to protect Brown. The jury found them guilty of threatening an FBI agent and intentionally impeding the feds' investigation in what had become a dangerous turf war.

At their sentencing, an angry US District Judge Percy Anderson told a packed courtroom that his ruling would not trivialize the defendants' actions. He scolded the defendants: "You have embarrassed the

CHAPTER 12

sheriff's department. None of you showed the courage to do what's right." He issued sentences ranging from twenty-one to forty-one months in prison.

The voters of Los Angeles County chose their next sheriff in a November 2014 runoff. Former Long Beach police chief Jim McDonnell garnered 75 percent of the vote. The other 25 percent went to Paul Tanaka, who was by then the subject of the continuing federal grand jury investigation into the FBI sting. In May 2015, Tanaka was indicted for orchestrating "Operation Pandora's Box," the scheme to keep the FBI from finding Brown. In the trial, prosecutor US Attorney Brandon Fox labeled Tanaka as the "ringleader from the beginning." In April 2016, a federal jury convicted Tanaka on conspiracy and obstruction of justice charges.

Before delivering his sentence to the eighth LASD official convicted in the FBI obstruction, Judge Anderson first gave Tanaka a "scorched-earth speech" according to those in attendance. His admonishments ranged from, "The most troubling thing about this troubling chapter in the sheriff's department's history is that your efforts to shield dirty deputies has been largely successful," to "Not only did [Tanaka] fail to identify and address problems in the jails, he exacerbated them." Anderson also described Tanaka's manner in court as "evasive, combative, and not credible." Federal guidelines for the dual crimes of obstruction of justice and conspiracy to obstruct justice ranged from forty-one to fifty-one months in prison. Judge Anderson gave Tanaka sixty.

For over a century, communities of color across the US had denounced police for their unjust practices, abuse of power, and unaccountability. Their accusations had fallen on mostly deaf ears. But in the years before Tanaka's conviction, their cries were beginning to be heard. In response to George Zimmerman's 2013 acquittal in the shooting death of Trayvon Martin, a Black seventeen-year-old, outraged Americans began using the hashtag #BlackLivesMatter on social media.

Zimmerman was not a law enforcement officer, but a movement had been born.

Had it not been for George Holliday's video, Rodney King may never have become a household name. Back in 1991, there was no such thing as a cell phone with a camera. But when a Black man, Eric Garner, lost consciousness after New York police officers pinned him on the sidewalk in 2014, a witness had recorded the entire event on his cell phone. Garner's final words, "I can't breathe," became a rallying cry and the nascent Black Lives Matter movement became instrumental in directing the national spotlight on officer-driven shootings of unarmed Black citizens.

A month later, a Black eighteen-year-old, Michael Brown, was killed by a white police officer in Ferguson, Missouri. What began as a candlelight vigil and peaceful protest devolved into mayhem, looting, vandalism, arson, and days of unrest between protestors and police in riot gear. When declaring a state of emergency and imposing a curfew in Ferguson didn't end the violence, the governor called in the National Guard.

In response to Martin's, Garner's, and Brown's tragic deaths—and the too many that came before and after—Americans of every race and creed demanded immediate and far-reaching police reform. Colin Kaepernick, a quarterback for the San Francisco 49ers, provoked further dialogue and endless controversy when he began taking a knee during the National Anthem in the 2016 NFL season. Kaepernick explained, "We have a lot of people that are oppressed. We have a lot of people that aren't treated equally, aren't given equal opportunities. Police brutality is a huge thing that needs to be addressed. There are a lot of issues that need to be talked about, need to be brought to life, and we need to fix those."

Anti-police sentiment in the United States had reached unprecedented levels. A Gallup poll showed that by 2015, Americans' confidence in the police had fallen from a 2004 high of 64 percent to

CHAPTER 12

52. Activists called for justice at any cost and propagated the message that "All Cops Are Bastards." "Contempt of cop" is a saying used in law enforcement to describe when someone is outright disrespectful and antagonistic toward them. But the expression falls short when officers have targets on their backs and, with no provocation but plenty of malice aforethought, are literally hunted down. This was the national climate at the time of the FBI's investigation into L.A. County jails and the ensuing trials.

In April 2013, Lee cooperated with US Attorney André Birotte, Jr., answering questions for over four hours about everything he had known in 2011 about allegations that his deputies had obstructed the federal investigation and subsequently threatened the FBI agent in charge. Lee had been given a letter of assurance that he wasn't the target of the government's investigation. But after witnesses implicated Lee in the 2014 trial of six deputies, the government believed it had caught the sheriff in a lie as to how much he had known about his deputies' sequestering of Brown and their harassment of the FBI agent in charge.

In Percy Anderson's court in February 2016, Lee pled guilty to a single count of making a false statement during his almost three-year-old interview. His other option had been to go to trial but, he had balked at the estimated $3 million debt he would incur in legal fees and didn't want to put his family through the trauma. Lee conceded that he had known about his deputies' plans to confront the FBI agent. In a plea deal between Lee's and US attorneys for the Central District of California that had taken months of negotiations, prosecutors agreed to a prison sentence of zero to six months, which aligned with federal sentencing guidelines for making a false statement in a federal investigation.

It was no coincidence that Anderson presided over the hearing. Initially, the case had been assigned to a different judge, but in February Anderson had successfully seen to it that the case was transferred to him. From the beginning, Anderson had implied that he thought Lee's six-month plea deal was too lenient and reminded the court that federal guidelines were just that—guidelines. The court could impose a sentence that included a cash fine of up to $250,000 and five years in prison, followed by three years of probation.

On July 18, 2016, the County Board of Supervisors was weeks away from finally awarding the contract to renovate the Hall of Justice, Lee's decade-long passion project. At the federal courthouse next door, in a resounding show of support, a throng of Lee's friends—ranging from a dear middle school friend to L.A. icon and former Dodgers manager Tommy Lasorda—waited for admission to Anderson's courtroom for Lee's sentencing hearing.

Lee's defense attorney, Michael Zweiback, emphasized that prison would be a cruel place for his client, who he disclosed, was suffering from Alzheimer's disease. Ever protective of his private life, Lee had wanted to keep his 2014 diagnosis private, but understood it may have been a factor in some of his decision-making. Zweiback quoted a letter from Lee's wife, Carol, in which she said, "There are all kinds of lost keys, and there have been lost keys for a variety of months now; that he loses his ATM cards, that he forgets his appointments, that he becomes frustrated when he can't remember his friends' names, that there are certain very basic things of recall we're talking about in recent past that he is unable to recall."

When Lee had been interviewed for over four hours back in April 2013, the lead questioner was US Attorney Brandon Fox. So it was unusual that Fox had been assigned to prosecute the case against Lee for one count of lying to federal officials (in other words, lying to him). In Tanaka's trial, Fox had stated that the government understood Tanaka to be "far more responsible" than Lee and that "[Lee's] crime is not as serious as the crimes by the members of the sheriff's department who were convicted of beating inmates and filing false reports

CHAPTER 12

in order to have people charged with offenses they did not commit." The prosecution's sentencing memo stated, "[Lee] issued orders that, taken literally, may not have been corrupt, but were carried out in an obstructive manner by his subordinates." Fox also added that in all the related obstruction cases, Lee had been the only defendant to admit to any wrongdoing.

At his sentencing hearing, Lee read a prepared statement:

> Your Honor, thank you for your time and consideration. I appreciate this significant task you have in presiding over my case. I am profoundly regretful you have had to give your attention to both my case and the other cases associated with the sheriff's department.
>
> I stand here today humble and filled with remorse for my mistakes as the sheriff of Los Angeles County.
>
> I have had the great honor of serving the sheriff's department for close to fifty years and leading it for sixteen. I was trusted by the people within the department and this county to provide leadership. I valued and honored that trust beyond measure. I took that task seriously.
>
> My life was dedicated in total to the community of Los Angeles, our great nation, and law enforcement community post 9/11. It is my entire life's work.
>
> I sought to improve the lives of the disenfranchised and disadvantaged. I worked to serve the entire public, including inmates in the jail system and sheriff deputies as well.

The Education Based Incarceration program that I started guided many inmates to better lives after their jail sentences were complete—to me, I know that I improved their lives, and that makes me very happy.

But as we are here today, I know that I failed. I have always prided myself in cooperation and leadership. Yet, in the investigation into the sheriff's department I did not lead; instead, I delegated the responsibility for this important duty, and I should not have. Moreover, I should have stood as the department's leader and taken control of the investigation. If I could do this again, I know I would do so.

I have always sought to overcome any challenge to help the community be stronger. Now with this diagnosis of Alzheimer's, I have an additional challenge ahead of me, perhaps the most difficult of my life.

I know that my family, friends, and public are with me as I face this challenge. I believe that I've always sought to overcome any challenge, Your Honor, to help the community become stronger. And I also felt that my family and friends and the public are going to help me with this, and I want to thank them.

Your Honor, you will sentence me today as the man I am now. I'm no longer the sheriff or a public official. I remain committed, however, to continue to get back to the community of Los Angeles for as long as I can, despite my current challenges. I'm only hopeful that in

CHAPTER 12

sentencing, Your Honor, you will permit me to do so. Thank you.

An editorial in the *Metropolitan News-Enterprise*, a daily that reports on the Los Angeles courts, described what happened next: "The judge excoriated Baca for his participation in witness tampering—notwithstanding that a position paper of the Office of US Attorney's said that the 'extensive investigation and multiple trials have revealed no evidence that suggests defendant Baca was ever aware of this witness tampering.' Anderson accused Baca of complicity in altering evidence, something not charged, not even hinted at by prosecutors."

Lee's future was in Percy Anderson's hands, and the judge's comments had done little to inspire confidence that his ruling would be fair and impartial.

The Robing Room is an online forum where lawyers with first-hand experiences rate judges on a one-to-ten scale on temperament, scholarship, evenhandedness, and more. At the time of this writing, Anderson's average ratings are 2 for temperament, 3 for scholarship, and 2 for his ability to handle complex litigation, with an overall assessment of 2.8. Comments describe him as "rude, dismissive, condescending, and unprofessional." "Unfortunately, your client will lose out with the judge imposing a higher retaliatory sentence even if the government requests a more moderate punishment," reads one comment. "He practically radiates arrogance, hostility, disrespect, and anger," reads another.

In 2011, the Robing Room included Anderson on its list of the ten worst US judges.

Before Anderson was commissioned to the United States District Court for the Central District of California in 2002, he served as a federal prosecutor in the same court and, later, on the 1991 Christopher Commission, which investigated the LAPD's use of excessive force in the Rodney King beating. Lee's team went into the hearing fully aware that Anderson was known for coming down hard on law enforcement. In defense of his bias against an LAPD police officer who had been nominated as top cop of the year, Anderson purportedly had said, "The LAPD shot too many people anyway." His judgments on Tanaka and the others had been harsh. Though Lee's team was hopeful in spite of Anderson's statements at the plea hearing, all were blindsided by the judge's decision on the plea deal.

The purpose of the hearing was for Anderson to issue a sentence on the charge at hand—how Lee should be reprimanded for lying to federal investigators—a charge for which he had already pled guilty. But Anderson rejected the prosecution's recommendation and all but admitted his own bias:

> Steps were taken by the defendant's subordinates to hide an FBI informant from the grand jury, records were destroyed and altered, including a federal grand jury subpoena, deputies were taught how to cover up abuses committed by their fellow deputies, how to look the other way, how to shield the department from embarrassment, all of which led to fostering an us-versus-them mentality, an unwritten code that taught deputies that when an inmate dared to attempt to harm a deputy, the deputies were taught to respond with enough violence to send that inmate to the hospital.
>
> While the guidelines chosen by the parties places no value on this type of harm, I do.

Lee had two options. He could maintain his admission of guilt and accept whatever sentence Anderson issued there and then, or he

CHAPTER 12

could withdraw his guilty plea and proceed with whatever course the government dictated.

Knowing Anderson could impose a sentence of up to five years, Lee withdrew his guilty plea, thus prompting a jury trial that began six months later. About his decision, Lee said:

> I made this decision due to untruthful comments about my actions made by the court and the US Attorney's Office that are contradicted by evidence in this case.... While my future and my ability to defend myself depends on my Alzheimer's disease, I need to set the record straight about me and the Los Angeles County Sheriff's Department on misleading aspects of the federal investigation while I'm capable of doing this.... I want to thank my friends and family for encouraging me to stand up for what is right. My spirits are high and my love for all people is God's gift to me.

Before the trial started, Lee's legal defense petitioned that both Anderson and Fox be recused on the grounds that Anderson had been prejudicial at the sentencing hearing and that Fox, a potential witness, was the investigator Lee had admitted to lying to. Given the level of Lee's celebrity in Los Angeles, they also requested a change of venue to another district in California. All requests were denied. On top of that, a grand jury added two more counts against Lee: conspiracy and obstruction of justice. Anderson chose to sever the three counts into two trials. The first would address conspiracy and obstruction of justice, charges that had not been included in the original plea deal.

On December 7, 2016, a jury was selected for *The United States of America v. Leroy David Baca* for obstruction of justice and conspiracy to obstruct justice. (For a detailed overview of the chain of events between

Anthony Brown's receipt of the contraband cell phone through Lee's guilty plea, see Appendix A, defense attorney Nathan Hochman's opening statement.) On the afternoon of December 22, after almost three days of deliberation, Anderson announced the jury had not been able to reach a unanimous decision and, to his great disappointment, he declared a mistrial. The jury had voted eleven to one in favor of acquittal. When interviewed later, one juror stated, "I don't feel there was any evidence that showed that Mr. Baca was guilty." Another described the loan juror holdout as biased against Lee.

Some thought that was the end of it, but in under three weeks, Fox announced the government's decision to retry Lee that February, this time for all three counts together: conspiracy, obstruction of justice, and lying to a federal investigator. In pretrial negotiations, Anderson added insult to injury, ruling that Lee couldn't wear his mini sheriff's star lapel pin or cuff links in court. He wouldn't let the defense introduce evidence of prior good deeds—such as EBI, the Jail Management Task Force, the OIR, and Lee's force prevention policy—that might relate to the charges at hand. He barred testimony from inmate witnesses favorable to Lee and from command staff who could attest to Lee's efforts to address jail violence. Further, Anderson forbade testimony related to Lee's Alzheimer's and rejected the defense request to unsever the three counts, significantly raising the stakes from the last trial. If found guilty, Lee would now face up to twenty years in prison.

The prosecution had previously named Tanaka as the ringleader of the plot to hide Anthony Brown and harass the FBI agent. Lee had first said he hadn't known of the plan, but then admitted to having peripheral information, but no details. In the retrial, the government argued Lee had "authored, monitored, and condoned" the conspiracy and assigned Tanaka to see it through. There was no evidence supporting such a claim. But with the inclusion of the false statement count, the prosecution was able to follow a different tact.

CHAPTER 12

It is worth remembering the court had denied the defense's request to recuse US Attorney Brandon Fox. With the three counts against Lee unsevered, Fox played for the jury the recording of April 2011 when *he* questioned Lee—when the sheriff had been assured he wasn't a target of the investigation. By barring Lee's entire interview with the FBI as evidence, Anderson had cleared the way for the prosecution to cut and paste the recording for the jury and delete important statements made by the sheriff. Juxtaposed with witnesses' statements, Fox brought Lee's character into question and suggested he had a sinister role in orchestrating the obstruction, despite there being no such evidence.

The trial lasted two weeks. After deliberating for two days, the jury reached a unanimous verdict, finding Lee guilty on all three counts. Lee was the tenth member of the LASD convicted for obstructing the FBI's investigation into the jails via Operation Pandora's Box.

With Carol by his side and the utmost dignity, Lee addressed the press outside the courthouse: "I want to say that I appreciate the jury system. However, I disagree with this particular verdict. Now, you've known me for a long time. I am a faith-based person. My mentality is always optimistic. I look forward to winning on appeal. . . . It's a privilege to be alive. That's how I feel. And I feel good."

Letters testifying to Lee's character and urging leniency flooded Anderson's office. They were from leaders of all faiths, current and former elected officials, law enforcement personnel, rehabilitated inmates, and the father of a slain deputy. One letter even came from a prominent civil rights activist, who listed a few examples of Lee's "long-running advocacy of constitutional policing and humane rehabilitation" and wrote, "Lee Baca consistently risked backing policing and rehabilitation visions that were ahead of his professions' status quo, and by doing so, he helped pave the way for their eventual acceptance."

At the sentencing hearing in May, the prosecution recommended a twenty-four-month sentence. But Anderson decided on thirty-six months, one year of probation, and a $7,500 fine. He added that if it weren't for Lee's medical condition and years of public service, he would have given him five years, as he had for Tanaka.

Anderson's animus toward Lee was unmistakable. So, it didn't come as a complete shock when Anderson denied bail and ordered Lee to go straight to prison. Lee's team immediately filed an appeal, which the Ninth Circuit Court of Appeals upheld.

When talking to the press after learning he would spend three years in prison, Lee was characteristically upbeat and matter-of-fact: "Today is an interesting day in the chapter of my life. I want to introduce you to my wife, Carol. This lady is actually one of the most persistent and supportive aspects of my life, because her life has been turned upside down with this matter as well. So, I want to thank you, honey, for the great work you do to help me as we continue our journey in life."

Lee's subsequent appeals to the Ninth Circuit and the US Supreme Court were denied.

The retired sheriff had been so accepting of the outcome that he spent the following weeks comforting his friends, rather than the other way around. A plea for a presidential pardon was already underway. Not knowing where the winds of fate would blow, Lee and Carol committed to living the fullest life they could. In July 2019, they flew to Michigan to attend longtime friend Lee Iacocca's funeral. From there they visited Niagara Falls. They returned to the East Coast that fall to see another friend, New York City Fire Commissioner—and later, Police Commissioner—Howard Safir, receive an award from the Drug Enforcement Administration. Though Lee had been to New York too many times to count, he had seen little more than hotel and conference rooms. He was delighted to see the city as a tourist and to follow up with a drive through the New England fall foliage. When he returned home to San Marino, he maintained a busy breakfast and lunch schedule with old friends and remained faithful to his morning runs.

Epilogue

La Tuna Federal Correctional Institution

"What I have is the ability of being positive when people are being challenged in a negative reality."

Lee was instructed to surrender at La Tuna Federal Correctional Institution in northwestern Texas during the first week of February 2020. A stone's throw from the Rio Grande and with the Guadalupe Mountains as a backdrop, the Spanish Mission–style prison was built during the Great Depression. Looking more like a grander and restored version of the Alamo, La Tuna is divided into two camps: low-security, and a minimum-security satellite for inmates who need less supervision. One of the most memorable events in its storied history was when con man and bank robber Benjamin Hoskins Paddock—described as psychopathic, egotistical, and arrogant—escaped in 1968. Paddock remained on the FBI's most-wanted list until he was caught ten years later. (In 2017, his son Stephen committed the deadliest mass shooting in US history when he killed sixty people at a country music festival in Las Vegas.)

Having received the order on short notice, Carol was unable to find a flight to El Paso. Three friends offered to drive her and Lee the twelve hours to La Tuna. Lee was in good spirits, hopeful he'd have time to tour El Paso before having to report. While they were on the road, President Trump declared a public health emergency. The coronavirus that had brought China to its knees had arrived in the US.

Carol had been Lee's constant companion for over twenty years and had never left Lee's side during the arduous ordeal that had stretched out for almost a decade. Lee had increasingly leaned on Carol as his cognition slipped away. Before their goodbyes, she left her cell phone number with a guard, unsure Lee would remember how to use a pay phone or even be able to follow the prison's procedures for making calls.

Ten days passed before Lee was able to phone Carol. After that, he called her almost daily. During their fifteen-minute conversations, Carol could tell Lee's memory was worsening. She was upset at being helpless to help him and guide him through his increasing confusion. It was a comfort that Lee remained as positive and active as ever. He still ran—though his routine had been reduced to three days a week—and did hundreds of kickbacks, push-ups, and squats every day. Intolerant of disarray, uncleanliness, and failures in maintenance, Lee volunteered to fix up the prison. After reorganizing the library, he tackled the grounds—clearing brush, renovating the pond, and rearranging the rocks in decorative patterns. Inspired by Lee's example, other inmates pitched in. When Lee wasn't exercising, working, reading, or napping (something he'd never had time for before), he was a friend to both the correctional officers and to the incarcerated. He counseled newcomers and those who struggled with their past, present, and future. Lee made many friends at La Tuna and when they were released he was never resentful or jealous. He celebrated with them. His time would come.

EPILOGUE

During his presidency, Donald Trump had issued 83 commutations and added 116 more in January 2021 before he left office. Despite family and friends' efforts to appeal to Trump, Lee's name didn't make the list.

Given Lee's age, Alzheimer's disease, and unmitigated lack of threat to society, he was the perfect candidate for a compassionate release. Carol tirelessly tackled the complicated application process. The week the seventy-seven-year-old began his sentence, the World Health Organization declared a global health emergency. Worldwide, more than two hundred people had died from COVID-19. As the pandemic grew, prisons soon became super-spreaders of the virus; at the end of 2020, the Marshall Project and the Associated Press reported one in five US prisoners had COVID-19, compared to the general population, where it was one in twenty. When the US Attorney General advised the Bureau of Prisons to maximize transfers to home confinement under the CARES Act, Lee's early release seemed likely.

The La Tuna warden submitted recommendations for Lee's early release to the Bureau of Prisons multiple times. And each time the request was denied with no explanation.

When Lee began his sentence, Carol had compiled hundreds of visitation requests from Lee's friends. But concerned about the pandemic, the prison had been placed on lockdown and no visitors had been allowed. Carol and Lee didn't see each other for sixteen months.

Lee's days hadn't passed without challenge. The air conditioning was too cold in the summer and the ninety-year-old building wasn't insulated enough to combat the winter temps, which could dip into the twenty-degree range. Lee was beset by a sore throat that lasted months. On top of that, he accidentally bit his tongue so badly it required stitches and took weeks to heal. COVID had disrupted normal operations with staff shortages, quarantines, and the closure of the cafeteria. Lee's dementia made it difficult for him to manage his spending account and purchase the items he needed from the commissary.

Despite the setbacks and the rejected appeals for an early release, Lee's spirits remained high. He encouraged those who served alongside him to make the most of their time, ensuring they return to society better educated and ready to do their part to make the world a better place.

With Lee's imprisonment, the ill-informed had celebrated that—in their mind—one of the nation's top cops had his comeuppance. It didn't matter that Lee hadn't been convicted of civil rights violations. It didn't matter that there was zero evidence Lee had authored the plot to hide an FBI agent. The average Angeleno didn't know that in Los Angeles County violent crimes such as murder, rape, robbery and aggravated assault had dropped 27 percent during Lee's last five years in office; property crimes, 11 percent. It didn't matter that Lee had fast-tracked changes in custody after learning everything his support staff had withheld from him. It didn't matter that inmates and sheriff personnel were better educated. It didn't matter that Los Angeles hadn't had a terror attack under his watch. As Lee himself acknowledged, "There's not a statement that says, 'Gee, the crime is at record low; there's more training, more supervision; the culture is education-based now; the inmate population is more subdued.' That never gets reported."

Were Lee's years in office without fault? No. And he would be the first to admit it.

Did Lee's conviction redress the misdeeds of others in law enforcement? No. Did the punishment fit the crime? No. One of the good guys had been unfairly laden with the sins of nameless others, those who had brought dishonor to the service Sheriff Lee Baca revered and upheld for almost five decades.

Lee was released to home custody on October 1, 2021.

Appendix A

Nathan Hochman's opening statement in Lee's first trial
December 7, 2016

On August 18, 2011, at around five o'clock in the afternoon, Sheriff Baca received a call on his cell phone from FBI Assistant Director Steve Martinez, the head of the Los Angeles office. Now, it was not unusual for Assistant Director Martinez to call Sheriff Baca because, as the heads of their organizations, brothers in arms, they were partners in the fight against narcotic traffickers, terrorists, arms, and gangs.

But this particular phone call, however, was unusual. It was unprecedented. On this call, Assistant Director Martinez told Sheriff Baca something that he had never told him even once in the entire time they worked together or at any time in sheriff's department history. Steve Martinez in this phone call told Sheriff Baca that the FBI had smuggled a cell phone into the sheriff's jails as part of an undercover operation, had done so without letting anyone in the sheriff's department or the sheriff know, and now had an inmate that might be in danger and was in need of protection. Sheriff Baca couldn't believe it. He couldn't believe it, so much so that you will hear Assistant Director Martinez say Martinez had to repeat it several times, because what he couldn't believe and understand is that the FBI itself had smuggled a cell phone into the jail.

This unprecedented act of the FBI involved what you will hear to be an extremely dangerous form of contraband. Now, contraband is something like a cell phone that is strictly prohibited and illegal in a secured jail, since a cell phone can be used like a weapon in a jail, because it can be used to plan crimes, arrange to actually kill witnesses, plan escapes, and smuggle drugs into the jail. The cell phone was given to a violent and dangerous inmate, Anthony Brown, who is working with the FBI and had just received a life sentence of 423 years.

Now, listening to this on Sheriff Baca's cell phone, the evidence will show that Sheriff Baca needed to know how big of a problem he had in his jails, how many deputies or inmates were involved, how compromised was the safety in the jail that he was personally responsible for. You will hear that Assistant Director Martinez would give him no details. No details.

For the next six weeks, the evidence will show that the FBI stonewalled Sheriff Baca in giving him the information to get to the bottom of what happened with the smuggled cell phone.

Now, Sheriff Baca, you will hear, set a very clear agenda of what he wanted done: protect Anthony Brown and investigate the smuggled cell phone.

You will hear that others went beyond that agenda, and that was wrong. But the evidence will also show that Sheriff Baca did not know, authorize, agree to, or condone any of those wrongful actions. The government talks about "they" over fifty times in their opening, but "they" did not include Sheriff Baca agreeing, condoning, authorizing, or knowing about those wrongful actions. Now, Sheriff Baca, you will hear, as the evidence in this case will show, had no problem at all with the FBI, the ACLU, or anyone else looking into his jails. No problem. He treated them all as partners if their intent was to make the jails better and safer.

Now, this case is not about civil rights violations, deputy beatings, or inmate abuse. It is not. Because while these are all very serious issues, none of them, none of them have been charged in this case. Instead, this case is about whether Sheriff Baca, in the six weeks following that August 18 phone call in 2011, agreed to and obstructed the FBI's investigation into civil rights violations, which the evidence will show he did not.

APPENDIX A

My name is Nathan Hochman, and along with Tinos Diamantatos and Brianna Abrams, we have the privilege and responsibility of representing Sheriff Leroy Baca.

You will hear how these six weeks in August and September of 2011 fit within the career of Sheriff Baca.

Sheriff Baca is seventy-four years old. He grew up in East Los Angeles and first served his country in the Marine Corps Reserves as a young man. He then spent the next forty-eight years of his life, almost five decades, serving the people of Los Angeles County in the Los Angeles County Sheriff's Department, including being the elected sheriff, the head of the department, being reelected three different times, and serving a total of over fifteen years as a sheriff of the Los Angeles County Sheriff's Department, until he retired in 2014.

You will hear that the focus of the evidence during these six weeks in August and September of 2011 is on one of the seven jails, Men's Central Jail. And the sheriff was in charge, not just of this one jail, but you will hear that his responsibilities stretch far, far greater than this just one jail. As a Los Angeles County sheriff, his territory covered over four thousand square miles from Long Beach to Lancaster, from Pacific Palisades to Pomona, the largest county in the United States, with ten million people in the county, an amount that's more than the population of forty states in the United States. He was in charge of the largest jail system in the entire country, a jail system that had a $2.4 billion budget that many . . . which is actually greater than many states' entire budgets. He is in charge of eighteen thousand inmates in seven different custody facilities. The jail has run the largest mental health facility in the entire country. They actually ran the largest homeless facility in the entire county. And the sheriff's department employed eighteen thousand people: nine thousand sworn deputies, nine thousand civilians, in twenty-three different patrol stations.

Now, you will hear, in addition to all that, the sheriff's department was the law enforcement provider. What that basically means is that certain cities, forty different cities, didn't have their own police, and they would contract with the sheriff's department to be their police. So, the sheriff was in charge of policing forty different cities, ninety different unincorporated areas, and other service areas including nine community colleges, fifty-eight superior courts, and the Metropolitan Transit Authority and the Rapid Rail Transit District that dealt with hundreds of thousands of people every day.

So, all this responsibility was on the sheriff's plate every day, but especially including during those six weeks that will be focused about in the summer of 2011.

Now, you will hear that the evidence . . . that the sheriff not only dealt with the incredibly busy activities of the sheriff's department, but he also met throughout the county, throughout those four thousand square miles, with community organizations, elected leaders, individuals, religious groups, nonprofits. He would even testify in front of the L.A. County Board of Supervisors, and he would even go to Congress to bring more funding back to Los Angeles County for law enforcement.

If that wasn't enough, Sheriff Baca, who regularly worked twelve- to fourteen-hour days, six to seven days a week, was a California Region 1 Director of Homeland Security, and that covered Los Angeles and Orange County, and was in charge of thirteen million people, and worked with not only the FBI but it also partnered with federal, state, and local agencies.

So, for over forty-eight years, Sheriff Baca worked at the sheriff's department. Those forty-eight years represent approximately 2,500 weeks. Of those 2,500 weeks, which you will hear about, is that we're just going to focus on six of them between August and September of 2011. So, forty-eight years, or 2,500 weeks, becomes six weeks. And then how much of the evidence in those six weeks will actually involve Sheriff Baca? As you will hear, it will be less than three hours of that

APPENDIX A

evidence. So, forty-eight years will go down to six weeks, will go down to three hours.

Now, how do we get to that August 18, 2011, phone call?

Well, the evidence is going to take you back over a decade when Sheriff Baca came in as sheriff. You will hear that there was an old-school way of dealing with inmates: warehouse them, get them in, get them out. Don't give them any skills while they're there because that's not part of our job, and if they come back, they come back. Well, what you will hear is that, when Sheriff Baca came in, he had a different approach to inmates. From the beginning, he himself drafted a statement of core values that was given to every member of the sheriff's department, and that emphasized respecting inmates rather than treating them as the enemy. The core values stated: "As a leader in the Los Angeles Sheriff's Department, I commit myself to honorably perform my duties with respect for the dignity of all people, integrity to do right and fight wrongs, wisdom to apply common sense and fairness in all I do, and courage to stand against racism, sexism, anti-Semitism, homophobia, and bigotry in all its forms."

The sheriff also adopted a new mission statement when he came in, and that mission statement highlighted defending the rights of all including the incarcerated. It stated: "Lead the fight to prevent crime and injustice. Enforce the law fairly and defend the rights of all, including the incarcerated. Partner with the people we serve to secure and promote safety in our communities."

Now, the evidence in this case will show that the core values and mission statements were taught in the sheriff's academy to up-and-coming sheriffs. They were posted in all those twenty-three patrol stations. They were posted in the jails. They were posted online. They were constantly emphasized by the sheriff when he was talking to the eighteen thousand members of the sheriff's department and when he gave hundreds of speeches to the public. The sheriff created policies, procedures, and programs to implement the core values and mission statements throughout the jails.

Now, as part of defending the rights of all, including the incarcerated, the sheriff sought out partners. And you will hear that one of those partners, starting all the way back when he took office in 1998, was the ACLU. And you will also hear, when the ACLU representatives testify, that the ACLU has been working with the sheriff's department for over twenty years at the time in 1998 when the sheriff came in. At this point it's over thirty years.

You will hear that the ACLU serves a vital and important role in the jail, a role that Sheriff Baca welcomed. You will hear that what the ACLU had, that basically nobody else had, was this thing called a monitor, a jailhouse monitor. And what is a monitor? The evidence will show that a monitor is an actual person who gets to go inside the jails, gets to talk to any inmate that they want to, gets to go into housing, the actual cell area—not the visiting area, but go inside the jail—that they actually have access to the court and they can report their court findings directly to the federal judge and that they actually issue annual reports to the public, a very unique role that the ACLU was partnering with the sheriff to monitor what was going on in the jails.

But the sheriff did not just rely on the ACLU to monitor the jails and tell him about the interactions between deputies and inmates. He also had at the sheriff's department two different bureaus. The first one is called the Internal Affairs Bureau. The second one is called the Internal Criminal Investigations Bureau. That's the IAB and the ICIB.

And what you'll hear is that the deputies who were employed in these bureaus had a full-time job to do one thing, and that was investigate allegations of any deputy doing something wrong. That was these people's full-time job.

So, the evidence will show that the sheriff was not afraid of having anyone look at those jails. In fact, what you will hear is that, in addition to the ACLU, in addition to the IAB, the Internal Affairs Bureau,

APPENDIX A

the Internal Criminal Investigations Bureau, the sheriff set up something that was unique, first of its kind in the nation, not just for the L.A. County Sheriff's Department but for any sheriff's department in the entire nation, and it was called the Office of Independent Review.

Now, the Office of Independent Review is, as its name suggests, an office that is independent of the sheriff and provides review, sort of like a watchdog organization. Now, OIR investigated allegations of misconduct by sheriff deputies, and they had something that was unique that made it a unique organization. They had real-time access to the investigations. What does that mean, "real-time access"? They didn't have to wait until the investigators did the investigation, wrote their reports, and months and months later, get some reports that they can then maybe look back into. What they were able to do was get the access as the reports were being written, which made OIR a particularly effective independent review of the sheriff's department. And what you will also hear is that they were actually also able to weigh in on discipline recommendations for deputies that committed wrongful conduct. Now, who led OIR? Was OIR, this Office of Independent Review, led by someone who is inexperienced, who would be a rubber stamp for the sheriff? No.

The person who led OIR from 2001 to the present is a gentleman named Michael Gennaco. You will hear him testify in this case. And who is Michael Gennaco? Michael Gennaco is a former federal prosecutor who not only worked for the United States Department of Justice civil rights division, but he was the head civil rights prosecutor for the Los Angeles US Attorney's Office, where these two prosecutors work. He was the head civil rights prosecutor of that office. That's who was brought in, one of the most accomplished civil rights prosecutors in the nation. And while he was a prosecutor, Mr. Gennaco brought numerous cases, civil rights cases, against police officers who violated people's civil rights by beating them or using excessive force. He knows the difference between what is excessive force and what is not, and he

SHERIFF LEE BACA

has prosecuted before. And now he and five other attorneys are the Office of Independent Review monitoring the sheriff's department.

So, he will testify that Sheriff Baca created the OIR and ensured that OIR had sufficient resources to do its job. And then what you will also hear is that the—when OIR would actually publish annual reports, many of those reports were actually critical of the sheriff's department. The sheriff invited the ACLU, OIR, and the public to bring him the good, the bad, and the ugly.

Now, the evidence will show that the ACLU was working with OIR, the sheriff's department, from 2001 to 2009 to address these problems. But in 2009, '10, '11, the ACLU raised concerns in reports that they publish widely. You will hear one of the ACLU's directors speak to you. Peter Eliasberg. What he will tell you is that, in addition to the chaplain, in addition to other ACLU people, Mr. Eliasberg published the ACLU's reports widely. He gave press conferences. He gave TV and radio interviews. He went ahead and filed these reports with the court in order to make sure that the sheriff knew this public information and so did the FBI.

Now, the evidence will show that the sheriff and his department responded with programs, policies, and procedures to deal with the ACLU's complaints of deputy abuse. And what is important to know—and this is very important—is that you will not be asked to decide whether the sheriff's programs, policies, and procedures were adequate, sufficient, whether they investigated quickly enough, whether they disciplined enough deputies, whether they could have put in different programs, policies, and procedures to deal with the ACLU's complaints that might have worked better. Basically, whether the sheriff could have done a better job in responding to these issues. You will not have to decide that, nor are you going to be asked to decide whether the sheriff is responsible for any particular incident or allegation of excessive force or deputy beating. These are civil rights charges, and this case has not charged Sheriff Baca with violating any civil rights crimes, not one.

APPENDIX A

Instead, this case is only about a much different issue of whether or not the government can prove beyond a reasonable doubt that Sheriff Baca conspired and obstructed a grand jury investigation during this six-week period, and only this six-week period, in August and September of 2011.

Now, as the ACLU is issuing its reports in 2010, you're going to hear that the FBI decides to investigate these allegations. You will hear that the FBI in Los Angeles has over eight hundred special agents, many of whom have decades of experience investigating these crimes. And who does the FBI choose to lead its investigation into this inmate abuse in June 2010? You will hear they choose FBI Agent Leah Marx as the lead case agent.

How many years of experience and years had she been at the FBI in June 2010? One year. This was her rookie year.

How many years of prior law enforcement experience had she had at that point? None.

How many civil rights investigations had she been a case agent for at that point? None.

And what about experience in the jails? Did she have any unique experience in the jails so that she would know how, basically, inmates and deputies worked in the jail? She had none.

How about undercover experience? You heard Mr. Fox talk to you—there will be undercover experience. How many undercover operations had she run at that point? None.

What you will hear is, instead—the evidence will show that she began her investigation in June 2010 and she started interviewing about twenty-five inmates over the next year. And she will testify that each time she interviewed an inmate, she would go down to the Men's Central Jail, she would show her FBI credential, she would then write the inmate's name down on the form, and then the inmate would be brought to her in a room. She didn't go in with an alias. She didn't try to hide her name. She didn't try to hide that she was from the

FBI or that she was from the FBI's Civil Rights Squad. Over and over and over, FBI Special Agent Leah Marx is writing her name, showing her ID, and showing the deputies at the jail that the FBI is talking to inmates, many of whom have made complaints against the sheriff's department for abuse.

Now, of the twenty-five inmates that rookie Agent Marx interviewed over that year, she selected one particular inmate to try to build her civil rights investigation around. Who did she select? She selected Anthony Brown. And who is Anthony Brown? Well, you will hear that Anthony Brown is a dangerous and violent criminal, that Anthony Brown had a criminal record dating to the 1980s, that Anthony Brown was convicted of a 2005 armed robbery, basically went into a bunch of banks with a gun and got caught. And then you will hear in 2009 he did it again. He went into three different banks in 2009, put his gun up against certain tellers and customers. And, as he will say, he was high on crack cocaine at that time and even fired his gun at one woman, barely missing her. This is who Special Agent Leah Marx, rookie Agent Marx, selected amongst those twenty-five inmates to build her civil rights case on.

And what happened in the middle of that investigation in June of 2011, before the undercover went—before Anthony Brown gets his cell phone? You will find that he is sentenced to 423 years. You will also hear that Anthony Brown, amongst other things, is a serial liar and, as Agent Marx will describe on the stand, a manipulator. This is who Agent Marx chose.

So, Agent Marx meets with Anthony Brown ten to twenty times at Men's Central Jail and along the way tells her that there are deputies willing to take bribes in order to bring in stuff. Well, what kind of stuff? Again, we're talking about contraband. And remember, contraband is something that, while on the outside might be particularly fine, like food—outside food on the outside, fine. You bring outside food, or you bring drugs, or you bring cigarettes, or even

APPENDIX A

pornography, or outside food into a secured facility, and it's illegal. It's strictly prohibited.

So, what's the other thing that's also strictly prohibited? A cell phone. And why, again, is a cell phone a problem? Because what you'll hear and the evidence will show is that, when an inmate wants to make a call to someone on the outside and they're in the jail, they have to use one of the jail's public phones, and those phone calls are recorded. You can actually hear what's being said. It's recorded. You can see what numbers are being dialed. When an inmate uses a cell phone, they're able to bypass the system. And if they can bypass the system, you will see that they can, and have in the past, used a cell phone to plan escapes, to arrange to kill witnesses in their cases, to smuggle drugs into a prison, and to commit new crimes.

Now, you will hear that Anthony Brown told Agent Marx that he knew of one deputy that could be bribed for cigarettes or outside food or a cell phone. Which one of those three things did Agent Marx pick? The cigarettes, the outside food, or the cell phone? Evidence will show she picked the most dangerous thing to introduce into a jail, the cell phone. But as Agent Marx will testify, she and her supervisors nevertheless decided to test out the cell phone and see what would happen with Anthony Brown, a dangerous and violent criminal who is sentenced to 423 years.

Now, as the evidence will show, Agent Marx's bribe plan was as follows: What she was going to do is have Anthony Brown lie to what they later determined to be Deputy Gilbert Michel. And what was that lie? The lie was that Anthony Brown, through his bank robberies, had $800,000 stashed on the outside. And what he wanted was—he wanted Deputy Michel to bring him a cell phone. How much would he pay him? He would pay $2,000 to bring the cell phone in and $2,000 every time he charged a cell phone and brought it back to him. He gave him a $20,000 bribe. And you will hear that Deputy Michel agreed to it.

But how are they going to pay the bribe, because obviously Anthony Brown in the jail doesn't have $2,000—or $20,000, for that matter. Well, what you will hear is Agent Marx cooked up the bribe plan, and the bribe plan was, in essence, that Deputy Michel would go ahead and be contacted by C. J. on the outside, and C. J. would arrange to get him the money and arrange to get him the phone.

Who is C. J.? Well, what Agent Marx did was she had an undercover FBI agent—and they call him C. J.—make the contact with Deputy Michel and do that in order to keep the FBI distanced from the cell phone and Anthony Brown in the Men's County Jail, because they did not want to connect the FBI to the cell phone because that could endanger Anthony Brown's life if he got it because it would show, if they found the cell phone, that he was an FBI snitch. And being an FBI snitch in the violent wing of Men's Central Jail was extremely dangerous, as you will hear, because of how the other inmates could treat you or the deputies that you're snitching on.

So, Agent Marx took two steps to try to distance herself. She brought C. J. in instead of herself, and she even used a prepaid cell phone that would not be connected with the FBI. But she made three rookie mistakes that connected the FBI to the cell phone and endangered Anthony Brown's safety.

To understand these mistakes, you have to go back to the month before August and September of 2011 to July 18, because what you're going to hear on July 18 is that Deputy Michel and C. J. finally got together on the phone and they struck the deal: We're going to make—two days later, on July 20, I will give you a bribe payment. They didn't call it a bribe payment—"I will give you cash, and I will also give you the cell phone, and you can bring it to Anthony Brown in the jail."

So that's what's decided on July 18. They have the meeting on July 20. But the evidence will show that on July 18, 19, and 21, something happened that did not happen before: the three rookie mistakes of Agent Marx.

APPENDIX A

What happened is that Anthony Brown in the jail is very anxious. He wants to get this whole thing going. So rather than wait until he gets a cell phone, he calls Agent Marx on those publicly recorded jail phones, and he calls her on her desk line at the Civil Rights Squad at the FBI building in Westwood.

Now, for the past year he had made those phone calls, and she had never actually taken them because she knows that would then connect Anthony Brown, who is making the phone call, with the FBI Civil Rights Squad. But on July 18, 19, and 21, she took the calls. And what you will hear is that on July 18, for instance, in a recorded call, Agent Marx talks to Anthony Brown about the transaction. You'll hear on July 19, Agent Marx tells him in a recorded call that the sheriff's department is recording, "You will have your phone soon. Then you can call whoever you need."

Then you'll hear on July 21, again, Agent Marx talks to Anthony Brown when he calls from the jail on the public phone and assures him that, "You're good. You're good." What is Anthony Brown good for? Well, you'll hear that on July 20, Deputy Michel showed up in a parking lot near the Men's County Jail to do the transaction with C. J. What you will hear is that C. J. gave Deputy Michel a partial payment of $700 and the cell phone. And how will the evidence show this? You will see that there were six FBI agents surrounding these two cars. And where was Agent Marx? She was in a plane overhead with three other FBI agents, taking high-quality aerial photos, one of which is on the screen in front of you, that were so good that you could actually see the transaction from thousands of feet above.

The FBI got their man, they got it all on video, and they arrested him for the bribe.

Well, you will hear that two of these three things occurred. The FBI got their man, they got it all on video, but they didn't arrest him. Instead, you will hear that Agent Marx let Deputy Michel go and bring that extremely dangerous cell phone into Men's County Jail to Anthony

Brown even though at that point, because of the July 18, 19, and 21 phone calls, that phone call could be connected directly to the FBI and put Anthony Brown's safety in danger. Inmates would know he was an FBI snitch, and deputies could know who was snitching on them.

Why did Agent Marx allow this? As the evidence will show, Agent Marx believed that the numerous dangers of having a cell phone in the prison was outweighed by the possibility that Anthony Brown would somehow be able to shoot videos or photos of deputy beatings that might just coincidentally occur right in front of his cell by somehow, I don't know, taking his cell phone, sticking it through the bars, and trying to video or photograph what was going on. That was the plan.

And what safeguards did Agent Marx use to make sure the cell phone wasn't used for some illegal or sinister purpose? Well, you'll hear Agent Marx testify that the FBI had a system that would allow her, if you plugged in a PIN number, to actually hear the call that's being made, or the text messages being sent as they were done. Did she use this system? No. You will hear that she could have set up an online alert so that, every time the phone was used to call or text, she would be alerted through her email. Did she do that? No. Was she—was she somehow otherwise able to listen to the calls or see the text messages being sent? No.

Instead, once the cell phone got into the jail, it did not go as planned. Anthony Brown's cellmate saw Brown with the cell phone, and he says to Anthony Brown, "Hey, I want to use that to call my girlfriend. And if you don't give it to me, I'm going to tell on you." So, Anthony calls C. J.: "C. J., can I do this?" C. J. calls Agent Marx, "Agent Marx, can we do this?" Agent Marx says, "Go ahead. Go ahead." Now, had Agent Marx known who the cellmate was at that time? The evidence will show no. Did Agent Marx know what crimes—remember, they're on the violent wing—the most violent wing of the Men's Central Jail. Does she know what crimes that particular cellmate was in for? No. Did she take any steps to then trace the calls that the cellmate used the

APPENDIX A

phone for? No. Did she even know if the cellmate had a girlfriend or is calling someone on the outside to do something very sinister with the cell phone? No. You will hear Agent Marx agreed to let this cell phone be used by the cellmate to call the girlfriend without doing any checks whatsoever. You will also hear that, at any moment in time, she could have just terminated the service for the cell phone so it couldn't be used, and she chose not to do that as well.

Instead, on August 4, you will see that there's a second bribe payment. Again, at this point they have another meeting in another parking lot. C. J. shows up with $800. So now you have a combined $1,500 for the bribe payment, and he gives that money on video, a dozen FBI agents surveilling. Once again, the FBI has got their man twice. They've got it on video twice, and they let him go again. When they let him go again, again, there are no provisions taken to make sure that the cell phone is not being used for a dangerous purpose.

Now, four days later (what you heard on August 8) is that the deputies found the cell phone in Anthony Brown's stuff, buried inside a glove inside of a Doritos bag. And Deputy Michel finds out almost immediately that the cell phone has been discovered, and he calls C. J. He says, "C. J., they've got the phone. You have to go get rid of your phone." He's panicked. He's very worried that they now found the cell phone. C. J. calls Agent Marx and tells Agent Marx the cell phone has been discovered on August 8 in the jail.

Now, the evidence will show that the clock is ticking before Anthony Brown is going to be found out to be an FBI snitch. Does Agent Marx go to the jail on August 8 or C. J. go to the jail and warn Anthony Brown that there can be possible repercussions or warn anybody in the jail that there could be possible repercussions? No. What you'll hear is they discovered the cell phone on August 8, and then from the 8th to the 23rd: August 8 to the 23rd, at no point from the 8th, 9th, 10th, 11th, 12th, 13th, 14th, 15th, 16th, 17th does Agent Marx or C. J. go to the jail to see how Anthony Brown is doing and let him know that the FBI is there for him. On the 18th, as you heard, it all comes out it's an FBI phone. At this point there's no reason not to go to the jail. But does she go on the 18th? 19th? 20th? 21st? 22nd? No.

You'll hear that the first time she goes is on August 23.

So then let me take you then back to August 18, because August 18 is when FBI Assistant Director Martinez calls Sheriff Baca to tell them about the FBI phone. What's also important to know is that why was it August 18 that Assistant Director Martinez is calling Sheriff Baca? Why didn't he call him on August 8?

What the evidence will show is that Agent Marx didn't even tell her boss, the head of the FBI's office, that the cell phone had been found on August 8, and he doesn't find out about it until August 18, ten days later. She keeps Anthony Brown in the dark. She keeps the head of her office, Assistant Director Martinez, in the dark.

Now, on the 18th, what you'll hear is that Assistant Director Martinez does make this call to Mr. Baca, and he provides him with the information of two points: The FBI cell phone has been compromised, and we've got to keep Anthony Brown safe. That's it. No more details.

Despite years of partnership, despite the fact that they had agents, there's sheriff's and FBI agents on twenty—over twenty sheriff's deputies are on FBI task forces. This is a partnership that had been working together for years. And despite that partnership, Assistant Director Martinez only provides Sheriff Baca with those two details. What did he not provide him?

The evidence will show that Assistant Director Martinez, for that six-week period, did not tell Sheriff Baca how the phone was smuggled into the jail, whether or not there were other FBI-smuggled cell phones in the jail that could compromise the jail security, whether or not there was other FBI-smuggled contraband. Maybe they were running multiple undercovers that the—in the sheriff's jails that he was personally responsible for the safety of. Is Assistant Director Martinez assuring him, "Look, this is the only one"? Not at all. Well, how many

APPENDIX A

deputies were involved? You know, at some point Assistant Director Martinez talks about Gilbert Michel, but he won't confirm or deny that there's other deputies that may be involved. How many inmates were involved? Well, they know about Anthony Brown, but is the FBI running multiple undercovers, compromising the safety of the jail? How big of problem was this for Sheriff Baca? Sheriff Baca—Assistant Director Martinez would provide him with no answers to these questions.

What you will hear is that Sheriff Baca had to begin his own investigation to find out the answers to these questions. And towards that end, he spoke with Undersheriff Paul Tanaka. Undersheriff Paul Tanaka, as you will hear, was in charge of the day-to-day operations of the sheriff's department, and he was the number-two person of the sheriff's department. And the sheriff talked to him on August 18. And on August 19, they had a briefing meeting with Undersheriff Tanaka and members of the investigative team. And it was decided then—at the last meeting—to have an August 20 meeting . . . so, a bigger meeting with Sheriff Baca, Undersheriff Tanaka, and the rest of the team. And this is going to be called the "Saturday morning meeting" because it's on a Saturday morning.

And what you will hear is that at that meeting, Sheriff Baca is very explicit as to what his agenda is, and there's two points on it. First, keep Inmate Brown safe, which is what the FBI had requested, and second, investigate how the cell phone was smuggled into the jail.

Now, you will hear about the relationship between Sheriff Baca and Undersheriff Paul Tanaka. When under—and what you will hear is that, when Undersheriff Paul Tanaka was in Sheriff Baca's presence, he was, "Yes, sir," "No, sir," "Thank you, sir." But when Undersheriff Tanaka was outside Sheriff Baca's presence, what you will hear is that he operated his own agenda. He had people that were loyal to him, not Sheriff Baca, and he often advocated the old-school way of dealing with inmates: warehouse them, get them in, get them out, us versus

SHERIFF LEE BACA

them, instead of Sheriff Baca's view that inmates were to be respected and rehabilitated.

Undersheriff Tanaka had not just the first point of the agenda or second point of the agenda, but you will hear that Undersheriff Tanaka added a third point to his agenda, something that Sheriff Baca didn't agree with, authorize, condone, or know about it: "F— the FBI." That was a third part of Undersheriff Tanaka's agenda, not Sheriff Baca's agenda.

So, over fifty times in opening statement, Mr. Fox referred to "they" doing something. "They," trying to group everybody together each time because it's "they." But what you will need to consider is what Sheriff Baca knew, authorized, participated in, agreed to—not what they did—because this case is not about "they." It is about Sheriff Baca.

Now, on August 23, you will hear how Sheriff Baca's agenda and Paul Tanaka's agenda clashed. On that day, as you heard, Agent Marx meets with Anthony Brown in the jails. She finally comes to visit them, and she meets with him for over an hour with two other FBI agents until Anthony Brown is taken out of the room by other deputy sheriffs. Now, when Lieutenant Thompson—Greg Thompson—that was on the government's chart, one of the sheriff's department investigators found out about this, he went to Paul Tanaka, and he said, "Mr. Tanaka, I'm sorry. The FBI went ahead and violated your order to keep the FBI away without your permission. I'm very sorry."

And what you will hear and see in an email is that Lieutenant Thompson had a "butt-chewing," quote/unquote, by Undersheriff Tanaka. They chewed his butt out, apparently, and was mad and angry that the FBI had been able to talk to Anthony Brown.

But what you're going to hear also is Sheriff Baca's response, because Mr. Fox told you about the incident. But what he didn't tell you, when Lieutenant Thompson went to go ahead and say the same thing to Sheriff Baca, is what Sheriff Baca's response was. And his response was

APPENDIX A

not angry at all: "Thank you very much"; unlike Undersheriff Tanaka's response, which was incredibly mad: "F— the FBI." Sheriff Baca's response was—because his agenda was not to keep the FBI at bay, keep them away—was not angry at all.

Now, as the evidence will show, what Sheriff Baca's agenda was, was to be open, transparent, and direct, the opposite of hidden, secretive, and deceptive. He had nothing to hide from the FBI or anybody else.

And where do we see that best? Well, Mr. Fox told you about a meeting on August 29. That's a meeting with someone called the United States Attorney. Now, the United States Attorney is their boss, the head of the United States Attorney's Office. He's not only in charge of Los Angeles County, but he's got all the six counties around it. They call it the Central District of California. That's Orange County, Los Angeles County, Riverside, and San Bernardino, Ventura, Santa Barbara, and San Luis Obispo. That's the United States Attorney, and that gentleman who you will hear testify, his name is André Birotte. Now, you will hear that Sheriff Baca scheduled a meeting with André Birotte, the very person who had the ability to bring conspiracy and obstruction of justice charges against anyone, and that's who Sheriff Baca meets with in person.

And the evidence will show that the purpose of this meeting, again, was to be open, transparent, and direct with the United States Attorney, and that's exactly what Sheriff Baca did. He told the United States Attorney—Mr. Fox calls it his displeasure, his anger—about the FBI inserting a very dangerous cell phone into the jail without his participation. And he proposed in this meeting that the sheriff's department work with the US Attorney's Office and the FBI in conducting their investigations. Again, they were partners in task forces. They had been partners for years. They could partner at this point because there's no more undercover investigation.

And what you'll hear is that Sheriff Baca made these points himself. He didn't send some underling, someone underneath him to make these points. He made them openly, transparently, and directly, and said the sheriff's department has the expertise with the jails for decades that the FBI lacks that we can bring into this investigation. And what did United States Attorney Birotte do? What was his response? He listened very politely, and he didn't engage in a dialogue at all. He didn't provide Sheriff Baca with the answers to any of the questions that Assistant Director Martinez wouldn't answer. He just sat there very politely, listening. And also, importantly, he didn't raise with Sheriff Baca that the federal investigation was having any problems like with a writ or anything else. So that meeting then was over.

And what next happens is that the evidence will show that many actions now occur between about August 25 and September 8. And all those actions, I ask you to consider whether or not Sheriff Baca knew about them, participated in them, agreed with them, authorized or condoned them, because the evidence will show it's not "they," but that Sheriff Baca did not do any of the above.

So, for instance, complying with the federal writ, not at all. The evidence will show Sheriff Baca didn't even know a writ was served, didn't know it was being complied with or not complied with. That will be the evidence. Anthony Brown having his name changed. What will the evidence show about Sheriff Baca's knowledge or agreement with that? Zero. How about Anthony Brown being moved from place to place? The evidence will show Sheriff Baca didn't know, authorize, or participate in that in any way. How about the issuance of that policy regarding the FBI visits? Again, Sheriff Baca wasn't involved in that policy, wasn't emailed on it, wasn't communicated with it at all. How about seeking that court order for the FBI's files? Was Sheriff Baca involved with that at all? No. How about telling deputies not to cooperate? Again, Mr. Fox called it "they." But will the evidence in this case show that Sheriff Baca was in any way involved or knew about deputies being told not to cooperate with the FBI's investigation? No. How about sweeping for FBI listening devices? Absolutely no evidence you will hear that Sheriff Baca was involved with that. And how about the surveillance of FBI agents ordering that surveillance? You will hear that Sheriff Baca wasn't involved with that. In fact, was out of the country at the time. In fact, the time period that he's out of the country was right darn smack in the middle of this six weeks. So, in the six-week period, he's out of the country on an international business trip. He's actually the keynote speaker at a counterterrorism conference outside the country between September 8 and September 21.

Now, on September 22, when he came back or around there, he has a meeting with the investigators and Undersheriff Tanaka, and the issue of whether or not they should go ahead and interview Agent Marx comes up. And you will hear that Sheriff Baca—because at that point, again, the FBI had provided no details to him whatsoever about their investigation—you will hear that Sheriff Baca okayed that interview. But what's also very important to listen to is that Sheriff Baca at no point told those investigators to threaten to arrest Agent Marx or to arrest her. He didn't give either one of those directives. His only directive was to go ahead and interview her because he had gotten no information from the FBI at that point in time.

Now, on September 26, what you will hear is that two things occur. The first is, as the government mentioned in their opening, Sheriff Baca appeared on TV on *Good Morning L.A.*, one of the Fox morning shows. He was actually on the show to promote a charity raising funds for the disease lupus, and the host asks him, while he's making his appearance, "What about this FBI investigation? What's going on?" And what you'll hear is that on public TV, Sheriff Baca is open, transparent, and direct. He actually answers the questions. And what does he say? He says, well, "The FBI lacks experience in the jails." You'll hear that he says publicly, "It's illegal to have a cell phone in the jails," which it is. You will hear that the sheriff has the responsibility to run the jails, and lastly, the sheriff was going to meet the next day with the FBI to talk about it. This wasn't some type of public pressure on the

United States Attorney. You will hear the evidence that you can't pressure United States Attorney Birotte with a public TV appearance. This is the United States Attorney, the head of the FBI office, and you will hear that they cannot be pressured. The evidence will show Sheriff Baca going on TV and openly, transparently, and directly stating his view.

Now, what you will also hear is that later that day, Sheriff Baca receives a phone call from Assistant Director Martinez. And what did that phone call say? That phone call actually wasn't mentioned by Mr. Fox. He told you—he showed you that little clip from the video where they approached Leah Marx. They had the two investigators, the guy going like this, approaching Leah Marx. But what he didn't tell you is that what happens thereafter is that Assistant Director Martinez calls up Sheriff Baca and says to him directly, "Are you going to arrest Agent Marx? Two of your agents just threatened to arrest her." Immediately, Sheriff Baca responds to him, "No. That was not the plan. We are not going to arrest her. We don't arrest FBI agents." And learned that those two FBI agents had not just done what he asked them to do, which was interview Leah Marx, but had gone beyond his orders, which was wrong. And as soon as Sheriff Baca heard about it, he assured Assistant Director Martinez it would not be happening.

Now, on September 27, what you will hear is that Sheriff Baca did have that second meeting with the United States Attorney Birotte, and this time the head of the FBI's office was also at that meeting. That's the Assistant Director Martinez. This is the clear-the-air meeting, because for six weeks, Sheriff Baca has gotten no answers from the FBI, no answers from the US Attorney's Office about how big of problem he has in his jails. So, what happens at this meeting is that you will hear that the sheriff was angry. And again, the sheriff did not hide his anger. It's not who he is. You will hear that. He was open, he was transparent, and he was direct to the United States Attorney, the man who had the capability of bringing charges against him for conspiracy or obstruction of justice and the head of the FBI's office. And he said to them

APPENDIX A

words to the effect of what Mr. Fox showed you about: "These are my jails, g—d—."; and, "I'm the g—d— sheriff." And then he said, "If you, the FBI, want to gun up"—and by that it means, if you want to go ahead and draw the line in the sand and no longer be a partner with the sheriff's department—"all right. That's not the way I want to deal with it. I want to be your partner. I've been your partner for decades. But you won't trust us. How are we going to trust you back?"

And at that point for the first time in six weeks, Assistant Director Martinez tells Sheriff Baca what had happened, why they went into the jails without bringing it to his attention, what the FBI's investigation was. And at that moment in time, you will hear the air was cleared. How did that meeting end? If you had just listened to Mr. Fox's opening, you would think the sheriff took out his gun. That meeting ended with these gentlemen shaking hands and agreeing to work together going forward in the future. And the sheriff understood that the US Attorney made it clear there was going to be a federal investigation. They didn't want the sheriff's department to play an active role other than responding to document requests. But that was okay because the air had been cleared in the September 27 meeting.

So, as you listen to the evidence over the next several weeks, the government will present you documents, audio, video, and testimony to prove their case beyond a reasonable doubt because, as the judge has and will instruct you, Sheriff Baca is presumed innocent until the end of this trial and into your jury deliberations, until or unless the government proves beyond a reasonable doubt that he committed any of the crimes charged. And when you consider the avalanche of emails, for instance, that the government is going to present, pay very close attention to whether or not Sheriff Baca is on the "To," the "From," or the "CC" or "BCC" line. Pay close attention, because you will find in these avalanche of emails that Sheriff Baca is not on any of these emails other than the two he receives from Assistant Director Martinez.

Pay also close attention to how many cell phone calls exist between

Sheriff Baca and the investigators during these six weeks. What you will hear is that there are about sixty phone calls between Undersheriff Tanaka, the man with his own agenda, and the investigators. And then during this entire six weeks, Sheriff Baca calls the investigators two times. And also pay close attention to what the witnesses are going to say about whether or not Sheriff Baca was at all involved with Anthony Brown being moved around, a federal writ being issued, witnesses being told not to cooperate. The evidence will consistently show that Sheriff Baca was not involved.

Instead, you will hear that Sheriff Baca was extraordinarily busy. He was working twelve- to fourteen-hour days, six to seven days a week, with that enormous responsibility that I described before in running the sheriff's department and dealing with the entire responsibilities of being a sheriff. You will hear that, when Sheriff Baca got involved with the investigation, as he pointed out, he was open, transparent, and direct, the very opposite of secretive, deceptive, and hidden—the hallmarks of obstruction of justice. The ACLU was his partner; the US Attorney's Office was his partner; the FBI was his brother in arms.

And the government will fail to prove beyond a reasonable doubt that the sheriff conspired or obstructed a grand jury investigation into civil rights violations as charged in this indictment. Accordingly, we will ask you at the end of this case to return the only verdict, the only verdict that will be consistent with the evidence presented, a verdict of not guilty on both counts. Thank you very much.

Appendix B

"No Job is Too Big and No Responsibility is Too Small" by Leroy D. Baca, from *To Lead, To Learn, To Leave a Legacy*, published by the Major Cities Chiefs Federal Bureau of Investigation National Executive Institute, June 2005:

As Sheriff of our nation's largest county serving ten million people, my responsibility for public safety requires constant action, innovation, strong core values, cutting-edge technology, [and] positive political partnerships at the federal, state, and local level. Also required is a daring to be different, no fear of criticism, transparency regarding our mistakes, full respect and cooperation with the media, and big ideas. Most important is the training of all my employees to be leaders who thirst for knowledge to do better. This permeates our thinking and actions.

By example, I teach my people to create ideas, celebrate diverse people, and establish religious harmony throughout the County. Our specific action-oriented achievements include but are not limited to the following:

- Our first order of business was to develop core values that prescriptively require all of us to address properly the legal, civil and human rights of all Americans.

Our Core Values:

As a leader in the Los Angeles County Sheriff's Department, I commit myself to honorably perform my duties with respect for the dignity of all people, integrity to do right and fight wrongs, wisdom to apply common sense and fairness in all I do, and courage to stand against racism, sexism, anti-Semitism, homophobia and bigotry in all its forms.

- We have trained ourselves to be leaders who excel in our work responsibilities no matter what they are. To accomplish this, we created a Deputy Sheriff Leadership Institute that all sworn and professional personnel jointly attend without regard for individual rank, title or levels of responsibility.

- We provide educational opportunity at work sites for all employees so they may attain bachelors, masters and doctorate degrees. To accomplish this, we created an LASD University in partnership with five public and private universities who use our facilities for classrooms. This learning efficiency also created reduced tuition for the 2,000 Sheriff's personnel who are enrolled.

- We thirst for cutting-edge technology. Although the Department has a Technical Services Division, key leaders have special responsibilities to seek new technical tools. We are currently developing, as an example, the radio car of the future.

- We protect civil rights as a duty. To accomplish this, I created the Office of Independent Review (OIR) comprised of six civil rights attorneys. This body monitors all criminal and administrative investigations from beginning to end. It also recommends discipline or corrective measures based on Department guidelines. Our investigative credibility has not been challenged since the OIR's inception.

APPENDIX B

- We have built an organizational culture that is consistently substantive and values human needs. We have mentors of employees who are in need of support, including psychologists and peer group volunteer counselors. Significant volunteer charitable activities are going on throughout all departments. We aspire to be the most charitable law enforcement agency in the nation.

- We have eliminated most of the negative aspects of bureaucracy. I manage from the middle down. I personally visit each of our seventy commands on a regular basis to listen to the complaints and concerns of our sworn and professional staff.

- Finally, we believe we can do it all. We have shaped the role of police work to that of universal social work that reduces human misery and crime. We are supportive healers of human despair within children and adults. We believe that, "No job is too big and no responsibility is too small."

Because of these practices and approach, the Los Angeles County Sheriff's Department is a hotbed of hundreds of successful activities and programs led by 14,500 leaders backed by a 1.7-billion-dollar budget, and growing.

Appendix C

"In L.A., Race Kills," by Lee Baca, *Los Angeles Times*, June 12, 2008

Conversations about race are fraught with emotion, confusion and controversy. But that doesn't mean we should avoid or sidestep the issue.

As a Latino raised in East Los Angeles, and as the elected sheriff of Los Angeles County for the last decade, I have seen many sides of the race issue. I have lived it, in fact.

So let me be very clear about one thing: We have a serious interracial violence problem in this county involving blacks and Latinos.

Some people deny it. They say that race is not a factor in L.A.'s gang crisis; the problem, they say, is not one of blacks versus Latinos and Latinos versus blacks but merely one of gang members killing other gang members (and yes, they acknowledge, sometimes the gangs are race-based).

But they're wrong. The truth is that, in many cases, race is at the heart of the problem. Latino gang members shoot blacks not because they're members of a rival gang but because of their skin color. Likewise, black gang members shoot Latinos because they are brown.

Just look at the facts. In February 2006, our jail system erupted into a full-scale riot involving about 2,000 black and Latino inmates at the North County Correctional Facility at Pitchess Detention Center in Castaic. One black inmate died and numerous others were injured. Through extensive interviews with participants, our investigation revealed that race—not gang affiliation—was the motivating factor.

Furthermore, we have evidence linking inmates who are known

APPENDIX C

as "shot callers" directly to street shootings based entirely on race. These shot callers at Pitchess and elsewhere are affiliated with gangs, to be sure, and in many cases they may give the order to kill a particular person or a member of a particular gang. But if that person or gang cannot be found the shot caller will often order the gunman to find someone—anyone—who is black or brown and shoot them instead. Gang affiliation does not matter. Only the color of the victim's skin matters.

I would even take it a step further and suggest that some of L.A.'s so-called gangs are really no more than loose-knit bands of blacks or Latinos roaming the streets looking for people of the other color to shoot. Our gang investigators have learned this through interviews in Compton and elsewhere throughout the county. L.A.'s gang wars have long been complicated by drugs, territory issues or money. Now, it can also be over color.

Race-based violence has even found its way into our school system, although no deaths have been reported. Some say it's always been there, but it certainly is rearing its ugly head now more than ever. Most recently, fighting broke out in May between more than 600 black and brown students at Locke High School in South L.A.

The racial divide is being driven by the ongoing population growth and demographic changes that have buffeted L.A. for decades. The perception that one group has more opportunities and advantages than another can lead to resentment, competition and, ultimately, spontaneous eruptions of violence.

So where does this leave us? How does this information help?

I have begun a process in my headquarters in which analysts are poring over data collected from various sources throughout the county to help us understand exactly what gang crimes are underway—and where—in real time. I call it a Gang Emergency Operations Center.

It's about more than just identifying problem areas and moving more police there. In fact, it is not a suppression model at all, but an intervention and prevention model aimed at ensuring that those who need social services get them. More important, it will serve as a fusion center for sharing information. Such centers—like the federal Joint Regional Intelligence Center, which combats terrorism—have more than proved their worth.

But as we gather this data, the race issue must be part of the equation—because if it isn't, we are not analyzing the data correctly. Crimes with a racial component must be categorized and studied to help us better understand the problem. Racial issues must then be addressed through education and awareness.

The problem of interracial violence is not intractable; we've made progress in other settings. I have seen it on a small scale in the Sheriff's Department's Domestic Violence Prevention Program in our jails.

It happened like this. Inmates with a history of domestic violence—sometimes known members of opposite gangs—were forced to attend this program or be remanded to custody for a significant amount of state prison time. Those who agreed to participate would sit together and discuss various topics of interest. They would eat meals together and live together in housing set aside for them.

The program was designed to address issues of domestic violence. But over a period of weeks, the participants overcame barriers by being exposed to those they were supposed to hate. They began to form friendships—friendships that, in some cases, have lasted outside the jail walls.

This may seem like an insignificant occurrence to those who are uninformed about gang life and racial tension. But it is not. People who would shoot each other as easily as kick a can were taking meals together, talking together and living together without violence.

The better we understand the crisis, the better chance we have of solving it. It is difficult to believe that something as simple as gathering information, analyzing it and then putting it into action—whether through suppression, intervention or prevention—will have any effect. But it will. It's a proven formula.

The unification of information, dispassionately collected and analyzed will lead us toward a disarming of the gang culture. And through disarmament, we will make the streets safer. And that's the whole point.

Appendix D

In Service to All

Lee had made an oath to serve the people of Los Angeles County. And he made time to serve on the board of directors for organizations close to his heart: Optimist Youth Homes and School, Puente Learning Center, De Mi Corazon Foundation, Peace Angels Foundation, Buenanueva Foundation, the Watts Cinema and Entertainment Center, EMEK Hebrew Academy, the Harriett Buhai Center for Family Law, Fight Crime and Invest in Kids, the Crime and Intelligence Analysis Program, the National Sheriffs' Association, the Major City Chiefs Association, the Major County Sheriff's Association, the Sheriff's Relief Association, the International Public Safety Association, the Board of State and Community Corrections, and the International Association of Chiefs of Police. He also served on the Congressional Affairs and Homeland Security Committee as well as the Board of Governors of the USC Alumni Association.

Sources

This book wouldn't have been possible without the cooperation of Lee and Carol Baca. Generous with her time and personal documents, despite all the challenges with Lee's Alzheimer's, appeals, and confinement, Carol provided primary source documents, including Lee's letters, writings, and personal documents. After Lee began serving his sentence, her emails to Lee's friends and family about his experiences at La Tuna were rich with personal anecdotes and memories and updates on his condition.

Lee's longtime friend and colleague Richard Weintraub graciously provided an early read and his insight and first-hand account were invaluable.

Sheriff Joe Arpaio was generous with his time and support.

The list of secondary sources is long, but some were particularly rich in detail. In her blog "Witness L.A.: Criminal Justice Journalism in the Public Interest," Celeste Fremon's thorough coverage of the trials and details of Operation Pandora's Box provided insight into the events as they unfolded. The same can be said of her series in *Los Angeles Magazine*.

Also helpful were the Kolts Report, the Semiannual Reports by Special Counsel Merrick J. Bobb and Staff and Police Assessment Resource Center (PARC), and the Office of Independent Review reports.

Many documents and publications are available on the LASD website, including: *Achievements: Sheriff Leroy D. Baca's Second Term in Office, 2002–2006*; *Contract Law Enforcement Services, January 2009*; *A Decade of Leadership*; *Education Based Incarceration: Creating a Life Worth Living*; *Executive Clergy Council Year in Review 2011*; *Fiscal*

SHERIFF LEE BACA

Year 1981–1982 Statistical Summary; Herzberg-Davis Forensic Science Center; The Leaders Behind the Star: Reflections on Leadership in the LASD; Manual of Policy and Procedures; An Overview of the Pitchess Detention Center, 2012; Police Diplomacy: A Global Trust; Public Trust Policing; Strategic Plan, November 1, 2009; and the *Year in Review* series, which is published each year.

The archives of the *Los Angeles Times*, which are available online for subscribers, were visited frequently. Other Los Angeles publications offered different coverage and perspectives, including the *Antelope Valley Times, Arcadia Tribune,* county of Los Angeles's *County Digest, Independent, Long Beach, Daily Breeze, Daily News, LA Weekly, Los Angeles Business Journal, Los Angeles Magazine, Metropolitan News-Enterprise, Pasadena Star-News, San Bernardino County Sun, Signal,* and *Valley News.* Many of these papers are available through a subscription to www.newspapers.com.

National newspapers and magazines and trade and university publications that were uniquely helpful in providing specific information include *American Criminal Law Review,* the *Atlantic, Building Design and Construction, Deputy and Court Officer,* the *Guardian,* Harvard University Press's *Public Policy,* the *Jewish Journal,* the *Journal of Forensic Identification, Pacific Standard Magazine, Police Magazine, Police Quarterly, Runners World, Smithsonian Magazine, Time,* and *the Washington Post.*

As this book was written during the COVID-19 pandemic, most research was conducted over the internet. It's amazing what you can find. Reading transcripts of hearings and trials can feel like you're inside the courtroom or the chambers of Congress. All of the following can be read online: *People v. Zammora et al.; Rosas, et al. v. Baca; Thomas v. County of Los Angeles; United States of America v. Leroy Baca;* the Hearing Before the Subcommittee on Intelligence, Information Sharing, and Terrorism Risk Assessment of the Committee on Homeland Security House of Representatives One Hundred Tenth Congress, Second

SOURCES

Session, September 24, 2008; the Hearing Before the Subcommittee on Intelligence, Information Sharing, and Terrorism Risk Assessment of the Committee on Homeland Security House of Representatives One Hundred Eleventh Congress, Second Session, March 17, 2010; the Hearings Before the Committee on Homeland Security House of Representatives One Hundred Twelfth Congress, First Session, March 10, June 15, and July 27, 2011; "Voter Information Guide for 1994, General Election"; California Ballot Propositions and Ballot Initiatives; A microfilm project of University Publications of America "Records of the Wickersham Commission on Law Observance and Enforcement," Guide Compiled by Randolph Boehm, Samuel Walker, consulting editor, 1997.

Thank you to the researchers and scholars who wrote the reports and studies below, as well as those who scanned them and made them available to anyone with a search engine:

- ACLU of Southern California and the Bazelon Center for Mental Health Law, "A Way Forward: Diverting People with Mental Illness from Inhumane and Expensive Jails into Community-Based Treatment that Works," by Sarah Liebowitz, Peter J. Eliasberg, Ira A. Burnim, and Emily B. Read, July 2014.
- American Civil Liberties Union of Southern California Foundation, "Report on Mental Health Issues at Los Angeles County Jail," by Terry A. Kupers, M.D., M.S.P., June 27, 2008.
- American University, "William H. Parker and the Thin Blue Line: Politics, Public Relations and Policing in Postwar Los Angeles," by Alisa Sarah Kramer, 2007.
- The Aspen Institute Homeland Security Program, "Los Angeles' Preparedness for Terrorism," by Clark Kent Ervin, July 2009.
- "August Vollmer and the Origins of Police Professionalism," by Gene E. Carte, October 1972.

- California Research Bureau, "Children of Incarcerated Parents," by Charlene Wear Simmons, Ph.D., March 2000.
- City of Los Angeles, "The Legacy of Redlining in Los Angeles: Disinvestment, Injustice, and Inefficiency: Finding a Path Forward in 2019 and Beyond," by Jamie Tijerina, March 16, 2019.
- City of Los Angeles Department of City Planning Office of Historic Resources, "SurveyLA: Latino Los Angeles Historic Context Statement," September 15, 2015.
- Conference Report, "The Gulf States, European & North American Law Enforcement Symposium: The International Perspective on Law Enforcement Cooperation," November 3–5, 2009.
- County of Los Angeles, "Report of the Citizens' Commission on Jail Violence," September 2012.
- Eastern Kentucky University, "Policing Political Upheaval in the 1960s and Today: Which Side are You On?" by Victor E. Kappeler, Ph.D., April 15, 2014.
- "The History of Policing in the United States," by Dr. Gary Potter.
- Human Rights Watch, "Testing Justice: The Rape Kit Backlog in Los Angeles City and County," March 2009.
- JFA Institute, "Evaluation of Education-Based Incarceration Programs Los Angeles County Sheriff's Department Jail System," by Dr. James Austin, Dr. Jerrold D. Green, Robert Harris, and Robin Allen, August 2013.
- Legislative Analyst's Office, "An Overview and Assessment of Los Angeles County's 1995–96 Budget Problem," by Elizabeth G. Hill, July 11, 1995.
- National TEW Resource Center, "Resource Guide Book One: TEW Concept and Review."

- Office of Inspector General, "Community Oriented Policing: Los Angeles County Sheriff's Department," March 2016.
- "Police Structure: A Comparative Study of Policing Models," by John Varghese, May 2010.
- RAND Corporation, "Long-Term Effects of Law Enforcement's Post-9/11 Focus on Counterterrorism and Homeland Security," by Lois M. Davis, Michael Pollard, Kevin Ward, Jeremy M. Wilson, Danielle M. Varda, Lydia Hansell, and Paul Steinberg, 2010.
- RAND Corporation, "Profiling Inmates in the Los Angeles County Jail: Risks, Recidivism, and Release Options," by Joan Petersilia, Susan Turner, and Terry Fain, September 2000.
- "The Sleepy Lagoon Case: Pageant of Prejudice," by Alice Greenfield, executive member of the Defense Committee, 1943.
- Stanford Law School, Stanford Criminal Justice Center, "The First 72 Hours of Re-Entry: Seizing the Moment of Release," by David Ball, Robert Weisberg, and Kara Dansky, September 2008.
- State of California Board of Corrections, "The State of the Jails in California Report #1: Overcrowding in the Jails," by Carol A. Kizziah, November 1984.
- "Strategic Segregation in the Modern Prison," by Sharon Dolovich.
- US Department of Justice Bureau of Justice Statistics Bulletin, "Jail Inmates 1986," October 1987.
- US Department of Justice, Community Oriented Policing Services (COPS) "Law Enforcement Best Practices: Lessons Learned from the Field," 2019.

The Los Angeles County Board of Supervisors has a media archive of its board meetings which includes videos and transcripts of the times Lee appeared there. C-SPAN archives include footage of Lee's testimony to the Congressional subcommittee in New York after 9/11 and more. The LASD's own YouTube Channel was informative, as was archived news footage from television stations KABC, KCBS, KNBC, and PBS, and radio interviews like Madeline Brand's in 2012 on 89.3 KPCC.

Those of us who haven't had the privilege of attending David Belasco's class at USC can visit his YouTube Channel, the Leap TV, and feel like a Trojan. All his interviews are well worth watching, including the one with Lee.

During COVID, the Los Angeles Public Library made it possible to order books online and pick them up by appointment at local branches. The following books were invaluable in the writing of this book:

- *A Badge, a Gun, an Attitude: 25 Years as a Los Angeles County Deputy Sheriff* by Dean Scoville
- *Biscailuz: Sheriff of the New West* by Lindley Bynum
- *The Denial of Death* by Ernest Becker
- *History of a Barrio: East Los Angeles* by Ricardo Romo, 1983
- *My Life as a Lawman: Memories of a Historic Era* by Sgt. John Kocis, LASD (Retired)
- *Police Administration* by O. W. Wilson, 1963
- *Six Gun Sound: The Early History of the Los Angeles County Sheriff's Department* by Sven Crongeyer
- US Department of Justice's *Policies, Processes, and Decisions of the Criminal Justice System (Criminal Justice 2000, Volume 3)*
- *Varieties of Police Behavior: The Management of Law and Order in Eight Communities* by James Q. Wilson

SOURCES

Last—and far from least—a big thank you to Robert Barbera and Mark Montgomery. Without their vision, interest in telling Lee's story, and generous support, you wouldn't be reading these words.

Karen Richardson manages the Mentoris Project. Her first book, *Harvesting the American Dream,* is a novel inspired by the life of winemaker Ernest Gallo.

www.ingramcontent.com/pod-product-compliance
Lightning Source LLC
Chambersburg PA
CBHW022007120526
44592CB00034B/535